# Green by Design

# Green by Design

## Creating a Home for Sustainable Living

### ANGELA M. DEAN

Gibbs Smith, Publisher
Salt Lake City

For Phoebe and Maxwell

First Edition
07 06 05 04 03     5 4 3 2 1

Published by
Gibbs Smith, Publisher
P.O. Box 667
Layton, Utah 84041

Orders: (1-800) 748-5439
www.gibbs-smith.com

Edited by Jennifer Grillone
Designed by Metze Publication Design
Printed in Hong Kong

Library of Congress Cataloging-in-Publication Data

Dean, Angela, 1969-
Green by design : creating a home for sustainable living /
Angela Dean.—1st ed.
p. cm.
ISBN 1-58685-172-1
1. Sustainable architecture. 2. Architecture—Human factors.
3. Architectural design—Case studies. I. Title.
NA2542.36.D43 2003
728'.37'047—dc21
                    2003007000

# CONTENTS

# ACKNOWLEDGMENTS

This book would not be possible without the contributions of designers and homeowners who have so beautifully made the concepts of sustainable design a reality. Thank you for sharing your experiences. You are truly an inspiration for others who yearn for a better way to live, both in their homes and on this planet.

To my husband, Tim Brown, who faithfully read and reread the text providing invaluable insight, thank you. You are my anchor in this fast-moving current of life.

Thanks also go out to Maria Foster (a.k.a. Ma), Steve Foster, Adam Vetter, and Katie Pearce-Sassen for reading the drafts and providing valuable suggestions, encouragement, and hope.

And finally, to *mia familia* for teaching me the true meaning of home.

# PREFACE

This book will not attempt to offer prescriptive solutions for designing the perfect home. The one-size-fits-all approach has been tried by many developers and builders with poor results. As each of us carry different histories, ideas, and preferences, the homes we occupy should reflect these unique characteristics. As a wise friend of mine involved with environmental education always says, "I don't tell people what to think; I teach them how to think." That is the goal of this book. By providing you with knowledge, inspiration, and the ability to ask the right questions (and understand the answers) I hope to send you on your path to creating a beautiful, environmentally responsible home that you can be proud to live in.

There are numerous books on green design already filling the shelves of the well intentioned. So why add another? Unlike others, which tend to focus on the nuts and bolts aspects of construction methods, this book intends to move you to action by giving you an understanding of the design and decision-making process as well as examples of completed case studies which have successfully carried out their visions. Much can be learned by the example of others who have paved new ground. I hope that their stories will give you inspiration and motivation to create a home you will enjoy for years.

There are many environmental terms being tossed about in the building industry: sustainable, green, high performance, natural, and ecological to name just a few. What does it all mean and what is the difference between them? In the end, it is rather irrelevant which term you use or how you get there. The end goal is the same. In this book I will use the terms green and sustainable interchangeably.

The most common definition of sustainability is "the ability to meet the needs and wants of today without sacrificing the ability of future generations to meet their own needs and wants." Some may point out that the obvious flaw with this definition is the fact that we can't possibly know what the needs and wants of future generations will be. In spite of that, we still need to keep future generations and their need for resources in mind. Our society has functioned on the notion that we have inherited the earth from our ancestors and have no obligation to the future. We need to begin thinking in terms of borrowing the earth from our children. This slight semantic difference represents a change in philosophy that can have very powerful effects on the way we treat our resources. When we borrow something there is an implication that we will return it in as good a shape as when we received it. We may even throw in a few improvements as a "thank you" for its use. We should think of the earth's resources in these terms. Many who support sustainability have taken on a philosophy, adopted from the Iroquois people, of a commitment to the seventh generation. This translates into approximately 150 years, long beyond our lifetime. Although this may be beyond the normal scope of our thoughts, it is the time frame in which we must think of sustainability.

Now, how do we define the concept of home? On a basic level it is the place where we live, eat, sleep, spend time with family, keep our things, and maintain our lives. Home means something different to each of us and it is that difference that this book intends to help you define. For some, it is a showcase for ego, for others a place of refuge. We may see it as a business decision or as the creation of a lifelong friend. The goal is to think beyond the obvious and look deeper within ourselves to create a place that is worthy of the resources of time, materials, and money required to build it.

The concept for this book is one that has been evolving for many years. There are a few specific events, however, that I can easily look back upon as a source of inspiration. The first occurred upon visiting the childhood home of my mother in the remote hills of southern Italy. The homes were built around a common court as families grew, providing a shared place to work, play, and socialize. My mother's home was built by my great-grandfather out of local stone and other resources and was the source of many fond memories later shared with my generation. While her home, along with many others, had been abandoned when the owners immigrated to the U.S., it has existed with amazing integrity for over 100 years.

Another landmark event for me was when I received a copy of *Shelter* from a friend during my undergraduate studies. This was an awakening for me to a more humane form of architecture globally and through time. I longed to be a part of this type of space making. Instead at school I was offered courses on high-rise construction, technical drawing, and environmental controls. At this time I also began exploring the Native American ruins of Southern Utah. In a quest for time spent in the great outdoors I found something more powerful: The understanding that humans and nature can coexist seamlessly. We have forgotten the art of understanding how to live with our environment because of our desire to control it. So, as I was studying the mechanics of architecture required in school, I was being entranced with lessons learned on the outside: the use of local materials, structures built by hand, solar orientation, land-use planning, and beauty.

These events along with others have led me to view perfection in my field as "humanistic architecture." It may seem inconsistent to use that term while discussing green design. Typically one thinks of humans as being the source of the problem, and that we can merely slow down our destructive ways. The connection between the two concepts is simply that one should build with compassion for oneself as well as for others. Yet rather than introduce another term, I will use green or sustainable design to encompass the broad range of issues with the understanding of a much deeper underlying theme.

Professionally, I am challenged with finding ways to create this timeless architecture as I attempt to incorporate new ideas into practice. The great architecture of the world took many generations of evolution. Likewise I will give myself—and others venturing out into this territory—time and patience to become masters of place. Setting out on the right path is the essential element.

We cannot determine the exact needs and wants of future generations, and I will not even attempt to speculate what each reader needs and wants. What I will do, however, is attempt to help you make decisions that will have a lighter impact on the planet and resources that we have borrowed from future generations. The ideas presented in this book are chosen to demonstrate concepts that each individual may translate into their own situation. This will take some effort on your part, but hopefully in the end, you will find it an enriching and enlightening experience. Have fun! ■

WHAT IS THE USE OF A HOUSE IF YOU HAVEN'T GOT A TOLERABLE PLANET TO PUT IT ON?" —DUANE ELGIN

# CHAPTER 1

# Design Intent

Design can be a powerful tool. It determines our movement through space, offers focal points or distractions for our thoughts, and controls interactions with others. This notion can work against us or for us. If we understand and take control of design it can enhance the possibilities of enjoyment of our spaces. Taken a step further, well-designed spaces can help us live more fully than we had imagined. The combination of intentional life-style with intentional design can have powerful results. Sustainable design is a means to achieve this goal.

## Establishing Goals and Vision

If we step back to the very basics of what we want, we may start to think about ideas that reflect the feeling of a home that we are searching for, not merely walls, roof, and floor. We may desire a beautiful home that will evolve with us over time. Or we may want space that is healthy to live in while protecting the natural environment. As we determine the goals of designing a home and the characteristics we want, we should not jump to conclusions about what we need, but should do a bit of soul-searching as a first step. The rest will come easily.

Functional considerations are typically at the forefront of our thoughts when planning a new home. At its most basic level, a house is a shelter for a certain number of people. The house becomes more as it is designed in a manner conducive to the life-style of its occupants. This is where function influences design. Our wish list should not begin with a set number of rooms and square footage. Too often the size of a home is determined by the maximum budget allowed. Some begin their design process with the assumption, "I can spend $200,000, so at about $100.00 per square foot that should get me 2,000 square feet." Then the design evolves from there. Instead, planning should begin with thoughts of how you would like to use the space, what sorts of activities will take place in different areas of the home, how you will display or store valuables, and so on. The size of the house may still be 2,000 square feet, but a process that is more thoughtful and deliberate will result in a space that is more satisfying per square foot.

Budget plays an important factor in defining goals. We may either commit to spending an additional amount to get all of the features we desire, or we may hope to save money through proper planning and execution. It is often assumed that building green will cost more, but this is not necessarily the case. Money can be spent unwisely whether or not you are building green. Green can cost more or less, just as conventional can cost more or less. Plenty of conventional homes have been built over budget or with misused funds. In either case, it takes determination, research, and proper planning to find optimal solutions that fit within a budget.

Budgets may be based on a variety of factors. There may be a set amount available to you, or you may just have a feeling about limits based on what you think a home should cost. From there you evaluate how your "wish list" fits within the framework you've established. It is the rare case where budget exceeds expectations. Perhaps you are the lucky one whose goals and budget fit precisely. If not, you will have to prioritize and decide what needs to be done now and what can be added later if and when more funds become available. If you are designing your dream home, you will likely be faced with the desire to do things the right way from the start, instead of skimping on low quality materials or workmanship that may need to be replaced or updated later. This is a valid consideration that may involve reevaluating your budget's bottom line.

## What Do I Need? What Do I Want?

Do not limit yourself with the status quo. How you live today will influence decisions about your new home, but it should not set limitations. If you cannot find a suitable site to build near work but can't bear the commute, why not consider telecommuting from a home office? If you look a step further, perhaps what you yearn for is self-employment doing meaningful work that you enjoy. In this way, designing a home can also mean redesigning your life.

What does "home" mean to you? Are you reminded of a favorite spot in a house? An apple tree which beautifully shaded the front porch? Sitting at the kitchen table enjoying the smell of supper being prepared? What about that small hiding spot behind the closet where no one could find you? Our concept of home is influenced by a combination of memories as well as visions of the future. We may be unable to pinpoint exact locations or details of past experiences that drive our preferences but they are nevertheless very real. These experiences can manifest themselves in very interesting ways. A woman whose new home was recently completed discovered just how powerful these experiences can be. She was amazed and delighted at the realization that without intending to do so, she had re-created the floor plan of her grandmother's house. Of course the style and materials were completely different but something about the size and placement of rooms just "felt right somehow."

## Dare to Dream

Unlike what the real estate and development trades would like you to believe, there is no law against breaking out of the mold of four bedrooms, three baths, and three car garage houses. Many families are not represented by the *Leave It to Beaver* family structure. We have split families, blended families, single parents, couples without children, singles, singles who share a home, aging individuals and couples, as well as couples with children. Since there is no shortage of the market-driven layout, why not produce an alternative that is more livable for yourself and others?

Even those designing custom homes are, and should be, concerned with resale value. We can't predict the future; we may actually have to sell our sustainable dream home for that great job in Rome. However, to go through the process of designing your dream home, which you plan on living in for the long term, with a voice in the back of your head shouting "resale, resale!" is like shopping for an engagement ring and buying two just in case you need another

TOO MANY PEOPLE SPEND MONEY THEY HAVEN'T EARNED, TO BUY THINGS THEY DON'T WANT, TO IMPRESS PEOPLE THEY DON'T LIKE." —WILL ROGERS

## Your Commitment to Green

- Save money and resources by saving energy
- Be energy independent
- Use home as a net energy exporter (producing more energy than the home demands)
- Build to last with low maintenance
- Save money and resources by using fewer building materials
- Help to drive the market for green building
- Create a healthy living environment for your family
- Reduce your personal impact on the community and planet
- Be a good neighbor
- Become more self-sufficient
- Live in harmony with your beliefs
- Set an example to others
- Use local materials and labor to support local economy

someday. You will spend more money than is necessary and will not give your heart entirely to the effort.

## Map Your Memories of Place

Take a moment to reflect on past experiences in a place that brought you joy. This is not a suggestion to copy a previous plan, but rather to re-create the feeling a certain space conveyed to you through your own personal solution. The following exercise may help you get off to a good start.

You are not attempting to replicate a particular building or place. Instead, create a map of experiences you remember and the qualities of the places where those experiences occurred. It should not be of any particular scale or size, but it should allow you to provide enough detail to be useful. A map may include such places as a private garden filled with sunflowers where you buried your pet frog, the stair landing where you would read books in the light of a stained glass window, or a bedroom where you would retreat and watch the rain dance on the trees outside. Perhaps you're remembering not-so-pleasant experiences, such as having to share a room with a younger sibling or having to do your homework alone in a room away from your family's activities. Experiences, good and bad, have had an impact on your concept of home. By recognizing the root of these concepts we take control of finding solutions that best suit our needs. This is an exercise that is useful on a variety of scales, from a particular place to the greater community.

## Define Your Commitment to Green

Establishing your environmental priorities from the start is essential to successful integration of those priorities in the final design. Green is not a menu of add-on options, but a design aspect that is integral to aesthetics, budget, function, health, and enjoyment. Considerations should be based on the scale and duration of impact to self, family, community, and ecological systems. While this may seem like a daunting task at the outset, once elements are broken down to their basic nature it will make your decisions easier.

While each project may not achieve the deepest shade of green, each step taken toward that end is worth the effort. The sidebar Your Commitment to Green, may be helpful in determining your environmental priorities. You may want to come back to this list after you have read this book and completed more research because there may be other items you wish to add.

## Considerations to Building Green

It is important to identify the barriers that keep us from "going green" so that we can find the solutions and move forward. Following are some typical barriers, along with suggested solutions. You should make your own list of barriers and solutions for your particular situation.

## Cost

"How much does it cost?" is such a simple question at first glance yet typically it only refers to first costs of construction and fails to consider other important cost implications. For example, in addition to construction costs there are life-cycle costs. These are the costs that take into account the initial installation as well as operation, use, maintenance, and replacement over the life of the house.

When considering life-cycle costs, environmentally responsible solutions win—hands down. Preferable products are those that do not require a large amount of maintenance, do not need frequent replacement, and can be reused, recycled, or disposed of easily and inexpensively. Many sustainable solutions can actually earn you money. Take renewable energy for instance. It is a given that you will use energy for the duration of time in your home. Through simple estimation methods, you can determine the amount of time until you have saved (in energy costs) more than you have spent (on system costs). Any use beyond that time is essentially a gain in savings for energy produced. The often overlooked aspect of this calculation, however, is that the price of energy is not fixed. Since it is usually supplied by nonrenewable sources, one can only assume that the cost will increase and your savings will likely occur sooner than expected.

While it is difficult to put a price tag on environmental impacts, it is well known that building has a cost to society as a whole. Our beautiful home may be contributing to smog, poor water quality, and depletion of natural resources, which in turn cause various health threats, social inequalities, and ecological damage. One might argue that the cost to prevent environmental and social impacts is priceless, making discussions of a dollar figure rather irrelevant.

Other intangibles with cost implications for building have to do with quality-of-life issues. How do we place a value on enjoyment? Do we select our food, clothing, cars, computers, and toys on the same measure as houses—what is least expensive? Perhaps your answer is yes. If so, you needn't put this book down, because green design can save you money. Using synchronicity in design (the ability to use one design measure for multiple benefits) to make cost-effective choices will allow each dollar spent to go even further toward accomplishing your goals. For example, a more efficient building envelope requires less mechanical heating and cooling. Another example is choice of flooring material.

● Carpet

Wall-to-wall carpet is a best-seller due to its low initial cost. But how often does it need replacing? What is the true cost over ten, fifteen, and twenty years? Regardless of the budget issue, you should consider health as well. Carpet harbors dirt and pollutants that are difficult to remove; under certain conditions, carpets may harbor mold and mildew.

● No flooring

By this I mean no additional floor material other than what is required structurally. Concrete is a good example. Concrete can be easily stained and sealed with environmentally friendly products.

It has endless possibilities of style and color options, and has the added benefit of being a great thermal mass solution for passive solar design. Concrete production is energy intensive, however, so careful evaluation of pros and cons is important.

### Wood Flooring Cost Comparison

Standard hardwood costs about $8.00 per square foot installed. Bamboo flooring, a green alternative, can be installed for the same cost or less. Regarding life-cycle costs, bamboo is more durable than standard hardwoods and will need refinishing and replacing less frequently. Bamboo is rapidly renewable (maturing in five years) so, unless your hardwood is from a sustainably harvested source, bamboo will often rank higher on environmental qualities.

Photo © Steven Young, Courtesy of TimberGrass

● Natural

Say "dirt floor" and people think of endless sweeping and dusting, but in reality an earthen floor is solid, stable, and cleanable. And besides a little sweat equity, it's dirt-cheap!

## Codes

Building codes have been developed and are enforced with the goals of protecting the health and life safety of building occupants. Unfortunately, there are occurrences where the code has actually prescribed methods that are detrimental to these goals. One example is the requirement for treated lumber in wood construction where moisture may cause deterioration. A standard industry solution has been to use chromated copper arsenate (CCA), which is now being phased out by request from the U.S. Environmental Protection Agency, which has recently labeled CCA as a hazardous waste with known toxicity and harmful effects. As in most cases, there are healthy alternatives that achieve the same goal without negative effects. With increased awareness and a shift in market demand, these products will soon become the new standard.

Green design can be accomplished using many standard and readily available materials and systems. Many features of a green home may even be undetectable to the untrained eye, allowing your home to fit in with just about any neighborhood context. As mentioned in the previous example, however, you must be aware of more appropriate options for meeting building code requirements and not just what is standard in the industry. As long as the material or system you are choosing has data to back up its performance expectations, you will have no trouble with approvals.

If you are planning to build with a system that has not been tried in your area, you may have a bit of legwork to do. The current codes are written in a manner to open the door for acceptance of alternative systems, however it is ultimately up to the discretion of the local building official. It is rather ironic that building methods and materials that have been used for centuries are now named "alternative," while more recent technology-based systems of synthetic and highly processed materials are considered "traditional." Nevertheless, I will use the term "alternative" as it is now used for simplicity. Many codes and standards have been, and are being, developed to handle such alternative methods as straw bale, rammed earth, and bamboo. Scientific testing performed in homes built with these materials provides quantifiable data to the building industry. Such testing usually requires verification of structural characteristics, fire ratings, and resistance to deterioration. If you are planning to venture into new territory, here are some suggestions that may make your approval process a smooth one:

● **Educate yourself**

It is most likely that what you propose has been done before. Take the time to gather information from books, specially written codes, case studies, and interviews with building officials who have approved such methods.

● **Get to know your building official**

Because approval of your proposal is up to the discretion of the local official, you will have to convince that individual. It is best to begin a relationship with the building official during your design process rather than to wait until the plans are complete to inform him or her of your proposal. Your personal relationship will make a difference in the amount of time and consideration your ideas are given.

● **Educate the building official**

Share the information you have collected. It is quite possible that through education, your building official may become the new local advocate for such an idea.

## Availability

Market demand greatly influences availability of products and services. Over the past ten years the building industry has responded to increased interest in sustainable options. There are small start-up companies that deal solely with promotion of sustainable products. And many material producers, who have historically provided less than ideal products with regard to the environment, have made major changes to respond to demand. These companies want to sell and therefore have placed many green products in the mainstream of the construction industry. Whether based on a change in the personal ethics of company controllers or on a desire to keep up with the competition, the end result is positive, with more options to designers and clients. Many companies have found that improving their environmental record also improves their bottom line. This happens in many ways, including reduced waste, reduced chemical use and environmental cleanup costs, and improved worker satisfaction and productivity, to name a few. Environmentally responsible products are becoming easier to find, as PR and advertising are commingled. The caution here is that there are many companies that "greenwash" to sell a product. Since companies usually only tout the benefits of their products, it is up to the consumer to be a smart shopper and filter facts from fiction.

## Time

Time commitment toward design is not just an issue of green design, but of good design in general. If you want a great home it will take additional time and effort. Why shouldn't it? You would expect as much if reading a great novel or preparing a special dinner. Your custom home is hopefully a lifetime—or at least long-term—commitment. Whether or not your goal is to build green, the design of your home deserves much more than a second thought. Time invested will be returned through enjoyment of your creation for years in the future. When talking about additional time, I am speaking strictly of the design and planning stages. When it comes to the actual construction process, no undue time will be added by building green. In fact, you should plan to spend more time planning and designing than on the actual construction phase.

## Maintenance

Because a sustainable home includes the use of materials and systems that will last longer, there is less need for frequent replacement, thus reducing wear and tear on the home. There is also less requirement of energy to operate the home.

## Aesthetics

The energy crisis of the 1970s brought passive solar design to the forefront. However, the styles that emerged during that time have since made people shy away from designing with solar in mind. The long, boxy structure with a shed roof created an uninviting presence to many, who determined that solar was just not for them.

Times have changed. You wouldn't consider buying an early version computer system, nor should you buy into the undeveloped ideas of those early solar homes. Through the design ingenuity of many, passive solar design has come a long way in terms of aesthetics. A design may express its solar function or it may call for a subdued response. In either case, more human elements are addressed to create a welcoming presence; new solar home designs provide a people-focused atmosphere while still maximizing the benefits of sun capture.

Other aspects of green design can be even more difficult to detect. A completed house rarely displays the quantity and type of insulation, the performance of its windows, or the healthy qualities of its finishes. Alternative energy systems such as ground-source heat pumps are buried, and heating and cooling systems are often invisible. While these features are enjoyed and appreciated by homeowners and visitors, they are not style-driven and therefore allow a plethora of design responses.

## Experimental

Many of the concepts that support sustainable building have stood the test of time throughout the world. It's just that many people in the U.S. have been distracted by emerging technologies as the "right way" to do things, so that proper consideration hasn't been given to the "best way" to do things.

## Knowledge

Knowledge is power. There are endless resources available from individuals who have paved the way in building sustainable homes (see Resources section). Most who have gone through the process are committed to reducing their impact on the environment and are willing and enthusiastic about sharing their experiences. Tapping into these resources allows you to learn from other's mistakes as well as successes. And once you go through the process yourself, you will be one of those who can contribute to others who want to build green.   ∎

## SUSTAINABLE FEATURES

- Minimize construction waste
- Minimize site impact
- Restoration with native drought-tolerant plants
- Integrated design process
- Building shell efficiency
- Operable energy efficiency
- Renewable energy use

- Passive heating and cooling strategies
- Use of salvaged and recycled materials
- Low maintenance
- Nontoxic finishes
- Hard surface flooring and finishes
- Heat recovery ventilator

ABOVE

*This terraced and multilevel design allows for southern exposure to all major living spaces. Solar control is accomplished with a combination of fixed architectural features as well as operable shading devices.*

FAR RIGHT

*The organic form of the music room, along with its planted roof, visually connects the space to the surrounding landscape.*

# MILL ACRES RESIDENCE:
# Use of Light

For many years, my wife and I envisioned a house that had environmentally sound features and that would be economical to build and live in. We also wanted a house on a stream with habitat for wildlife and the opportunity for us to enjoy viewing it. Ideally, this house would also be close to work and/or public transportation," home owner Robert Plachta says.

While Robert and Nancy were unable to find an existing house with these conditions, they did locate the perfect site, complete with a creek, good wildlife habitat, and plenty of solitude. In addition to these natural resources, the site offered close proximity to work, shops, recreation, and public transportation, which minimize commute times and environmental impacts.

To them, an environmentally friendly home began with an understanding of and respect for the site and its natural resources. The goals were to minimize impacts to vegetation and desirable natural features, enhance opportunities for flora and fauna to flourish, and maximize the use of resources such as sun, wind, water, and earth. The building's design responds by nestling into an existing disturbed location and reusing a portion of an existing structural shell to preserve established vegetation. Site repair was also implemented with the planting of native, drought-tolerant turf grass that

replaced a large deck and pool, which had inhibited both views of and access to the creek. Waste wood from the demolition and construction process was chipped for use as mulch on site.

As a family of three with differing functional needs, they were inspired by the design principles espoused by architect Sarah Susanka in *The Not Too Big House* as a way of keeping the home at a reasonable scale with a high level of detail. They desired private spaces that offered intimacy and an open living/dining/kitchen area for family and entertaining.

### Site

The site is an oasis of life within a suburban context. Mill Creek offers aquatic life, while mature gamble oak, pines, shrubs, and fruit trees provide food and shelter for mule deer, belted kingfisher, and other wildlife. The gently sloping site offers a great deal of privacy. The house is surrounded by sounds of the rippling creek and wind through the trees, making for an easy escape from the bustle of the city just a few miles away. The climate is temperate; site conditions provide for great solar opportunities as well as wintertime buffers from cold winds. Natural breezes that flow through the site along the adjacent creek are tapped for internal cooling strategies.

A one-bedroom house on the property, built in 1954 of concrete masonry,

**Location:** Salt Lake City, Utah
**Architect:** Angela Dean, AMD Architecture
**Owners:** Robert Plachta and Nancy Carlson-Gotts
**Square Footage:** 3,300
**Cost:** $420,000
**Builder:** McCarthy Custom Homes
**Photographer:** Scot Zimmerman

provided little functional space and poor relation to the site. To reduce demolition waste and the demand for new materials, the foundation and concrete masonry shell were incorporated into the new design. Other elements such as decking, doors, and fixtures were salvaged for reuse where feasible. The new design's verticality minimizes site impact and provides solar access and views from all living areas.

An existing gravel parking area provided an appropriate location to install the ground source heat pump loops, while limiting new disturbances to the site.

### Process

Design decisions were based on benefits they offered in terms of function, aesthetics, and sustainability. One example is the stair tower, which functions as the home's circulation spine, entry point at mid-landing level, plenum for air movement, and path for natural ventilation through high operable windows. Another example is the material innovation that was accomplished with a formulation of concrete that allowed for a 1.5-inch concrete topping slab over wood framing, which serves as the finished floor. This solution also provided optimum heat transfer for the radiant floor system and passive solar strategies. By incorporating the existing shell, waste production and resource demands were reduced. It also provided beneficial thermal mass on the interior.

As with many design decisions, choices are usually a matter of weighing the costs with the benefits. Choices such as the ground-source heat pump, for instance, were a relatively easy sell. Since the owners plan on staying in the home for the

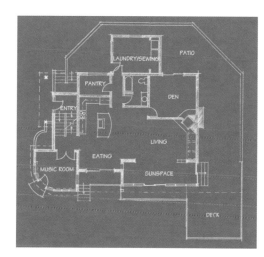

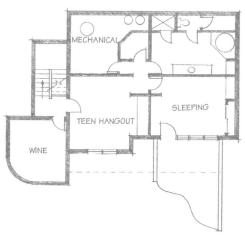

**ABOVE**

*A small alcove off the main living area provides a semiprivate space, while maintaining a connection to the rest of the household.*

**LEFT**

*From within the music room, the owners have sweeping views of the site. This spot serves as a quiet retreat, while remaining accessible. Natural light nourishes plants to soften the boundary between indoor and outdoor space.*

duration, a payback of five to seven years for this system was a sensible choice. The PV installation, on the other hand, was put on hold while awaiting expected legislative action initiating a tax incentive program for renewable energy.

After the design was complete, came the reality check of the contractor's cost estimates. Analyzing costs gave the owners an opportunity to define what elements were most important to them. In this case, they gave up a portion of exterior deck and reused more existing fixtures from the original structure to cut down on costs.

**Design**

The design solution resulted in a form that cascades down the sloping site, allows for solar access, offers expansive views toward the creek and mountains beyond, and has an interior that is open and airy while still providing quiet places for individual retreat. The use of ecologically sensitive materials, such as locally salvaged timbers and siding, created its own aesthetic that reflects the owner's eclectic tastes in furnishing and décor. Inspired by the vivid colors of Venetian architecture, they wanted to blend those colors with the play of natural light throughout the home. The home functions as an extension of the landscape, providing opportunities for plants to flourish indoors and outdoors—on terraces and balconies, as well as on the rooftop with a "living" roof of native plantings.

Interior living spaces expand outward to take advantage of the spectacular location. The home's functionality needed to respond to a family that wanted an open common area to enjoy each other's company while also providing the opportunity for solitude (computer games and music for the teenager, music and views of nature for Robert, plenty of outdoor lounging spaces for Nancy). The result is a "public" space that is centrally located, with "parent's zone" upstairs and "teenager's zone" below.

### Energy

Many options were investigated during the design process, in order to strike a balance between environmental considerations, functionality, economics, and practicality. The building is heated with both sun and earth, with passive solar heat as a primary source and radiant heat supported by a ground-source heat pump as a secondary source. The creek provides cooling breezes through the site, which are incorporated by the size and placement of operable windows. Additional techniques and equipment employed include a super-insulated building envelope, interior thermal mass, and energy efficient lighting.

The construction drawings were evaluated for Energy Star ratings and scored a five star, the highest score possible. Evidence of the home's efficient design was demonstrated during the city's record hot days of the 2002 summer. While the valley broiled, the house remained comfortably cool without the use of mechanical means.

### Water

The ground-source heat pump provides efficient backup cooling. Wastewater from the rooftop cooling unit is channeled for use in watering the "living" roof system. Efficient appliances and fixtures throughout the home make the most of energy as well as water resources. Waterwise landscaping, including buffalo grass, sage, and a variety of native wildflowers, provides for a gentle transition between structure and nature.

### Passive Solar

With primary views of the creek and mountains to the south, it was easy to accomplish

passive solar design while also capturing the view. The home's verticality enables sunlight to reach all living areas. A combination of shading strategies was utilized. Sizable overhangs were designed for maximum winter and minimum summer gain, and a retractable awning offers flexibility of control into the sun space. Light shelves wrap the west, south, and east elevations. These provide sufficient shading to the lower portions of glazing while allowing for high windows that capture views of Mount Olympus. They also throw daylight further into the interior as it is reflected off the light shelf's surface. In the master bedroom, high operable windows on the north wall provide for natural cross-ventilation. There are minimal windows on east, west, and north elevations in an effort to minimize heat gain and loss.

Thermal mass is an important element in passive solar design for heat distribution and reduction of temperature swings. The existing concrete masonry walls were insulated on the exterior to provide thermal mass where it is

RIGHT
*The home carefully nestles into the site, preserving existing gamble oak. Built-in planters and a "living roof" ease the transition between the landscape and the building. Locally salvaged wood timber and siding provide warmth to a simple form; the vivid colors were inspired by Venetian architecture as well as the changing seasons.*

most useful, on the interior. The colored concrete floors and countertops also provide mass.

### Materials

New walls utilize advanced framing techniques with 2 x 6s at 24-inches on center, and floor and roof joists are built with engineered lumber, each of which reduces the number of trees used in the building. Recycled fiber cellulose insulation fills the wall and roof cavities. An additional 1 inch of exterior insulation installed over the entire structure provides a thermal barrier and tight building envelope.

The "living" roof over the music room is planted with native drought-tolerant vegetation. This provides a visually pleasing view of the house as one approaches and can also be appreciated from the third story. Functional benefits include added insulative qualities of the earth, and the prolonged life of the membrane roof beneath. The remainder of the roof is surfaced with a white membrane that provides optimum solar reflectance, reducing heat gain.

"Trestlewood," salvaged locally from the Great Salt Lake, is used extensively both indoors and out. Interior stairs and trim, as well as exterior siding, trim, posts, and beams of wood create unity throughout the project. Stucco walls, pre-finished aluminum-clad windows and doors, and "Trex" decking (recycled composite lumber) provide a low maintenance exterior.

### Indoor Environmental Quality

With the tightening of the home's building shell to achieve energy efficiency, it was important that no harmful substances enter and that fresh air be supplied at a healthy rate. By leaving the concrete floors exposed, eliminating the need for carpet, this home avoids opportunities for dust particles to accumulate and

contribute to poor air quality. Healthy, non-toxic, durable finishes were specified throughout and an energy-recovery ventilator provides for the exchange of stale air for fresh without high-energy costs.

A detached carport is another design solution that contributes positively to indoor environmental quality. By eliminating the physical connection between the home and carport, car fumes have no chance of entering the living space. This also reduces the chances of oils being tracked in by the occupants.

"We look forward to living in the home for many years and anticipate incorporating additional features as time, budget, and opportunities present themselves. For example, we want to add photovoltaic panels and construct certain built-in items such as bookcases," Robert and Nancy say.

The owners have created a place they will call home well into their aging years. By striving for quality over quantity, goals of sustainability are achieved. Less space means fewer resources to build, maintain, and operate. This enabled the owners to invest in greater detail, giving the home a richness they appreciate every day. ■

ABOVE

*The ultraefficient fireplace provides more than comforting ambiance. It is an efficient, low-emission heat source that uses the waste wood salvaged from the construction process as fuel. Skylights adjacent to the fireplace, over the built-in bench seat, bring daylight further into the space. Exposed roof beams and the rich colors of the finishes provide a playful backdrop as sunlight moves through the space.*

**Location:** Northern Utah Mountains
**Architect:** Jack Thomas Associates
**Owner:** Anonymous
**Square Footage:** 3,000
**Cost:** Not available
**Builder:** Gordon Hellstrom
**Photographer**: Jan Stevenson

# SIMPLE STRAW:

# Living with Simplicity

The owners' goals for a new home evolved throughout the design process, which became not only a process of designing a home, but also a process of redefining their personal vision of life itself. They began with the typical approach of hiring an architect, looking at examples, and thinking about style and size. The initial parameters called for an approximately 5,000-square-foot mountain home. Little did they know that two years later, they would begin construction of a straw bale home of approximately 3,000 square feet (the required minimum in the community).

Throughout the design process they began stripping away elements of their life that seemed unnecessary. They wanted to be selective about the problems they faced on a daily basis and felt that simplifying the space around them could help in this regard. This involved removing clutter, both physical and psychological.

Their goals evolved into the desire to create a space that reflected this idea of simplicity. They were also taken with the idea of straw bale construction as a material that beautifully expresses the integrity of the structure. The style of the home would be influenced by the owners' desire to respond to the western vernacular of the region and to use recycled, and if possible locally available, materials.

**Space**

The couple desired a space that fit their needs, along with a bedroom for occasional houseguests. This meant a significant reduction in square footage from their original target. This was a risky endeavor. Most homes in the area are in the 6,000+ square foot range, which endures for several reasons, including market pressure for resale. The owners shunned this notion and decided that since they were spending their time and money, they were going to design a house meant for them. Besides, they believed that if it were done well, a potential buyer (should they ever sell) would appreciate the home's unique and well-crafted design.

ABOVE RIGHT

*The structural system of this home is expressed with locally salvaged timbers, which are visible from the outside in. Straw bale walls are fit within this system to provide a comfortable, natural, and efficient home. In this mountain setting with heavy snowfall, wide overhangs protect the straw bale walls from moisture.*

## SUSTAINABLE FEATURES

- Efficient utilization of space
- Minimized size of home
- Salvaged timber and stone
- Straw bale construction with natural plaster
- Simplified living through design process
- Daylighting strategies
- Energy-efficient building envelope
- Radiant heat

FACING

*The gentle curves and soft edges of the finished walls create a sense of calm. Radiant heat within the concrete slab further enhances comfort.*

The end result is a home that feels quite spacious, due to several thoughtful design strategies. The volume of space changes throughout the home, responding to the functions within. The vaulted ceiling remains a constant but the floor level rises from the kitchen/dining/living to the private areas, compressing the height of rooms. The open kitchen/living/dining configuration allows for a great deal of flexibility between dining for two or entertaining for twenty. Though not large, the kitchen is designed for optimum functionality. Years of experience in the restaurant business made for easy decisions by the owner when it came to work space, storage, appliances, and materials. The space is well organized, easy to use, and easy to clean.

### Materials

Exploring the alternatives to conventional construction reveals a world of opportunities. Beyond the choice of straw bale, the owners became interested in including other sustainable materials, such as natural finishes and salvage materials. The owners and architect traveled extensively looking for salvaged materials that could be used for the structure. They came across some fantastic trusses that were salvaged from an industrial building in Portland, Oregon, but upon further inspection and testing, the trusses were deemed unsuitable. What they ended up with was found "in their own back yard," thirty miles away to be precise: reclaimed timbers from an old Union Pacific Railroad trestle. These timbers provide for the post-and-beam structure as well as custom trusses that support engineered roof joists. The straw bales then act as an infill. Bamboo stakes rather than steel rebar were used to reinforce the straw, and the walls are finished with lime plaster to provide a breathable wall system that is resistant to cracking. Interior walls, including demising walls, are also lime plaster to match the exterior walls and to give continuity to the look and feel of the home.

Exterior walks and patios are made of maintenance-free sandstone. Ironwood decking, which is essentially indestructible, finishes the balcony off the master bedroom area. Plastered walls, salvaged timber posts and beams, and pre-finished aluminum-clad windows and doors are low in maintenance. The durable plaster is finished with two coats of natural, pigment-tinted lime wash for color and tone. The salvaged timber has aged, and will continue to do so, revealing its unique qualities.

Exterior door thresholds are made of sandstone curbs that were salvaged from a city street redevelopment project in 1989. Redwood found in a Portland salvage yard in 1990, originally salvaged from dismantled wine fermentation tanks in California, was used for the ceiling finish. Out of affection for these materials, they were kept for an opportunity, such as this, to arise.

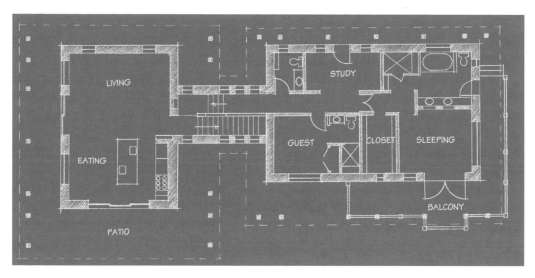

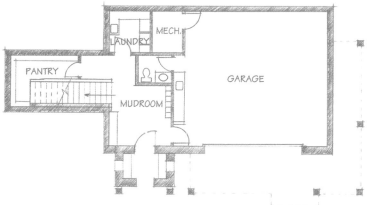

### Construction

This is the second permitted straw bale structure in the local jurisdiction and the first designed by the architect. The architect's main concerns with this building system were based on structural stresses of the region, which included a significant seismic zone and extreme snow loads. These hurdles were overcome with the engineering of the post-and-beam system, which acts as a moment frame, to resist these forces. The architect felt that the most important aspect of taking on a project such as this is a commitment to the learning curve. This, along with the desire to please the client, enabled him to pull off a successful project.

The owners were deeply involved in the construction process. To them, the beginning of construction did not necessarily mean the end of design. On the contrary, as the form took shape, new opportunities were revealed. The bale walls, for instance, were held short of their original plan to extend up through the gable ends. This gives the large volume of the kitchen/living/dining space a more human scale and reduces the number of bales and the amount of the subsequent plaster needed. Places were found for openings in certain interior walls to produce a fun effect with light. The interior walls were held short of the ceiling vault, again reducing the materials required.

### Energy

Due to the highly insulated walls, floor, and roof, the thermal performance of this building is exceptional. In addition, the window area is minimally placed where needed for framed views and daylight, which reduces potential heat loss through glass.

The building is oriented to the southeast, allowing morning light and heat to enter. Large overhangs protect the windows from solar gain as well as the walls from weather.

The design of the interior walls dictates that most terminate below the ceiling level. This provides a continuity of space and allows air movement through the home, which is useful in distributing heat and enables natural ventilation and cooling.

Hydronic in-floor heating is set into exposed concrete floors. This provides the most efficient heat transfer and eliminates the need for additional resources for finishes.

When asked why the walls remained unadorned by art, the owners reply, "We are just appreciating the beauty of the plastered walls—their rich color and texture." The place is minimally furnished as well. In response to their desire to simplify, they are adding one element at a time as they feel the need. For instance, a stereo and bookshelf is planned for the living space, which will join the couch and chair. Without apology they simply say, "We're quite comfortable with what we have chosen to surround ourselves with—our home, our belongings, our friends." By embracing the best of the best, they are truly living an intentional life-style. ■

TAOS RESIDENCE:

# In Harmony with Nature

After an introduction to the philosophy and design methods presented in a Permaculture design course, taught by Bill Mollison and others, the owners were motivated to live in a manner consistent with these ideas. Permaculture espouses the belief that through conscious design and maintenance of productive ecosystems, one may provide for food, energy, shelter, and other material and nonmaterial needs in a sustainable way. This notion inspired the owners to purchase land in northern New Mexico where they could put these ideas into practice and begin a more intentional life-style, which they instinctively knew would be rewarding.

Their design goals included a small, easy-to-maintain house (that could be extended later if necessary) made from

FACING

*Earth-plastered walls and an adobe fireplace respond to vernacular ways of building while the expansive windows are a modern transformation, allowing for light, warmth, and views.*

BELOW

*The construction of a new home provided an opportunity to restore a damaged and degraded landscape. By living sustainably on this site, the owners demonstrate that humans and nature can be compatible partners on the planet.*

**Location:** Taos, New Mexico
**Architect:** EDGE Architects
**Owner:** Anonymous
**Square Footage:** 1,350
**Cost:** $150,000
**Builder:** EDGE Construction Management
**Photographer:** Dick Spas

## SUSTAINABLE FEATURES

- Permaculture design
- Restoration of degraded site
- Constructed wetlands for wildlife habitat and aquaculture
- Compact size
- Local building materials: adobe mud, straw bale, Rastra block, cob interior wall, and light-clay interior wall
- Compost waste
- Gray water use
- Rainwater catchment
- Passive solar
- Natural ventilation
- Natural, nontoxic finishes

energy-efficient and renewable materials. Aesthetically it would respond to traditional styles of the area, blend with the natural surroundings, and take advantage of views of Taos Mountain.

### Design

The owners initially contacted an architect from Santa Fe who was also a permaculturalist. This seemed like a great fit and they set out to hire him. After much iteration over a complicated contract that he had presented, they decided that they just didn't feel secure with him and continued their search. They also recognized that it would make far more sense to hire someone from the Taos area who was familiar with working with local construction crews. Ken Anderson and Pamela Freund

of EDGE Architects came highly recommended by an old friend who described them as bright, young, and hungry. Their experience with alternative technology and building was a great benefit. They hit it off right away and were able to work with a simple and straightforward contract.

"We were deeply involved with the design process because we were in love with the whole place—Taos and our land. The idea of building in an environmentally friendly way was something we were inspired and determined to do," the owners say.

### Site

At an elevation of 7,000 feet, the temperature in the area varies by 40 degrees daily with summer highs of 93° to winter lows of –20°.

The site is a nine-acre piece of land that was an overgrazed pasture with a boggy area in the center. Federal grants from the Partners for Wildlife program enabled the owners to dig five interlocking ponds that receive water from the acequia system; the water is aerated and cleaned before it joins the Rio Lucero and a new acequia system begins. "We needed and wanted to have as low an environmental impact as possible," the owners explain.

The home is sited for optimum solar orientation and shelter from prevailing winds; it also takes advantage of mountain views. Outdoor spaces include a north porch facing the nearest mountains for hot summer days and a south patio where the owners can soak up the sun on winter days. A large pond near the home provides warming and cooling

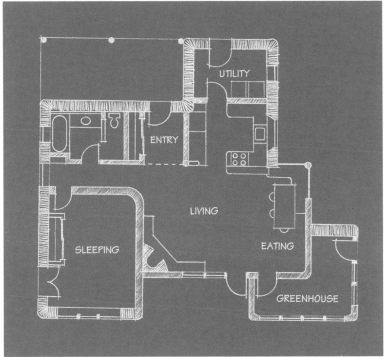

effects, with the attendant pleasures of hearing its rippling sound.

### Water

With a rainfall of ten to twelve inches per year, water scarcity is an issue that had to be addressed through efficiency strategies. A gray-water system, capturing water from kitchen and bath use for reuse in the landscape, is stored in an engineered mound north of the home. *Canales* (scuppers draining the roof) are located in such a way that runoff from the roof waters the garden beds and, in excessive rains, flows to the ponds and lawn.

Because of the site's high water table, they opted against a standard septic system, which could potentially contaminate the water. As an alternative, they installed a composting toilet (a Biolet from Sweden) with the added benefit of conserving water that would otherwise be flushed away.

### Materials

The residence utilizes straw bales and local adobe mud to create a comfortable, healthy, and sustainable small home in a high-desert climate. The clients were supportive of the architect's notion of using recycled and natural materials whenever possible.

Due to the site's high water table, it was necessary to elevate the home on a built-up structural pad above a French drain system. This made the foundation a more expensive part of the construction than usual. For foundation walls, they used Rastra block forms, a stay-in-place concrete form made from recycled Styrofoam and cement.

The wood post-and-beam structure uses hybrid box columns at openings. Six-to-eight-foot spacing allowed the use of smaller structural members, which resulted in fewer large mature trees being cut and transported. Also, people could lift the materials into

ABOVE, LEFT
*In the bedroom, a darker and more tranquil feeling was desired. This is accomplished by plastering the walls with a mud and mica combination and by installing an adobe floor.*

FACING PAGE, RIGHT
*Interior walls are built for heat storing capabilities using adobe brick and cob. In other areas, light clay walls provide sound insulation.*

FACING PAGE, LEFT
*With an average of twelve inches of rainfall per year, water efficiency is a high priority on this site. Gray water is captured from the bathroom for use in the landscape. A composting toilet manages the waste without the use of water.*

place and manipulate them without fossil fuel–driven machinery, such as cranes. Decorative wood columns were salvaged from a nearby forest that had recently experienced a fire.

The straw used for the walls came from approximately an hour and a half's drive north where barley is grown for a national beer brewery. Enterprising farmers bale the leftover straw for the home-building market. While they don't have the pollution problems from straw burning that California and Idaho suffer

from, they do grow more straw than can be used agriculturally.

Interior walls are built of heat-storing mass materials such as adobe brick and cob where walls are exposed to direct sunlight. In addition, light-clay walls provide sound insulation in other areas. Finished with gypsum plasters, the walls are bright and light in the public areas, and darker and more tranquil in the bedroom where natural mud and mica were used. The owners say, "Organic materials allowed us to create organic, human-scale

shapes and gave us a balance between hard and soft. We wanted the house to express its handmade nature."

The concrete floor was colored using a common fertilizer that provided an iron pigment. While they would have preferred the softness of adobe floors throughout, the expense of hired labor required them to limit the installation. They felt that it was important to create a natural, "womb-like" space in the bedroom, so extra money was spent for the natural adobe floor and mud plaster in that room.

A local cabinetmaker crafted the kitchen cabinets from pine that was reclaimed from a project in Texas. The countertops are durable, poured in place, colored concrete.

### Energy

Straw bale infill provides high insulation levels of at least twice what is required by code (R-42 is provided. while only R-19 is required). Because of high daily temperature swings, night-cooling techniques are effective at maintaining a steady, comfortable indoor temperature through the summer. Maximizing passive solar heating, supplemented with back-up radiant floor heat set at 68°, helps keep winter indoor temperatures steady. To avoid the use of chemically produced insulations, the roof is insulated with recycled, formalde-hyde-free cotton and cellulose to a value of R-60 (local code requires R-38). The attached green-house serves a double role as growing space and heat source for the house.

Energy- and water-efficient appliances and fixtures were used throughout the home. The refrigerator is a Vestfrost from Denmark, which is extremely energy efficient, and almost silent. As an added benefit to the environment, every part of it is recyclable. The front-loading wash-ing machine conserves both energy and water. Two Aquastar on-demand water heaters pro-vide the domestic hot water and the radiant under-floor heating.

The house is not off the grid since there was already electricity to the property prior to the owner's purchase. However, because they do plan to convert to a photovoltaic system in the future, they have chosen a gas stove and oven, as these will not be a heavy draw on the system once installed.

### Space

A ceiling that slopes from 12 to 15 feet high in the living area gives the home a spa-cious feeling despite its smaller size. This allows for a loft above the entryway. Views are spectacular in all directions. The bedroom faces south and is softened by earth floor and walls, which makes the room more quiet and restful. There is mica in the plaster, which pro-vides a subtle reflection of light from the walls. It has taken the owners more than two years to hang any pictures because they have been appreciating the walls as they were.

"Besides being extremely comfortable, with a very even temperature year-round, and very quiet because of the straw bale walls, the house gives us a lot of pleasure because there are few sharp angles. We enjoy the archways, curved walls, and rounded edges every-where," the owners say.

### Indoor Environmental Quality

With the exception of the front door, which is finished with a Bioshield product, the home is completely devoid of paint. Interior wood is finished with linseed oil and the concrete floors and countertops are maintained with beeswax.

The total cost was within budget at a little over $150,000. The owners attribute this to the careful work of their architects, who man-aged the construction process. ■

ABOVE
*The interior volume of space is opti-mized with a loft over the entryway. A tree trunk serves as structure for the loft while also proving a place to hang your hat.*

FACING
*The covered porch provides a place to greet people or to get out of the elements. The post-and-beam details of the porch enclosure hearken back to the vernacular way of building in the area.*

# CHAPTER 2

# Design Process

There are basic notions about good design that may be used throughout your green-by-design process. They include the desire to connect to nature, to provide a healthy environment, and to use resources efficiently and effectively. Good design also stands the test of time.

What is the definition of aesthetic? Beauty? Design? The answers are personal and often less a conscious thought and more an innate sense of what is right. I believe this innate sense is possible within all of us.

THE SIGNIFICANT PROBLEMS WE FACE CANNOT BE SOLVED AT THE SAME LEVEL OF THINKING WHERE WE WERE WHEN WE CREATED THEM." —ALBERT EINSTEIN

We say something is *natural* when it makes sense, has purity, and expresses meaning to us. We use the term *unnatural* when things just aren't quite right. One way to bring the sense of the natural into architecture is the idea of form following function. Green design encourages simple solutions that express the purpose and integrity of the building. A cupola used for natural light and ventilation also creates a special space where your vision and thoughts can soar. Large overhangs for passive solar control create a protected outdoor extension of space and anchor the building to its site. Rather than hiding structural elements, these may be brought into the forefront as finishing elements that eliminate the need for many additional embellishments. In these ways, sensibility is expressed through the physical structure.

Balance is another important element of good green design. Too much of a good thing can leave a bad taste in your mouth. Truly sustainable design utilizes a holistic approach so that a sensible solution can emerge. It wouldn't make sense to specify 100% recycled products in your home if their composition uses energy unwisely. Nor would it be sensible to focus primarily on energy savings if you were creating a trap of chemical soup on the interior that made the occupants sick. There are no clear-cut answers to this balancing act. Each unique project calls for a unique solution.

## The Process of Design

On occasion clients will enter my office with a plan in hand accompanied by an elevation drawing—something they have clipped from a magazine perhaps. This is intended to be a time-saver. They like the plan but "can the bedroom move to the north side, add another dormer there, enlarge a window here?" This approach leaves out many considerations such as relationship to site, views, and solar exposure; the lifestyle patterns and needs of your family; quality of space; and budgetary considerations. What soon emerges is awareness that there is more to designing a home than fitting rooms together within a given square footage.

While it is useful to gather examples of places that inspire you for use in the design process, the cut-and-paste approach to design does not work and will not address your needs and wants appropriately. If you're going to have something tailor-made, you will have much better results if it is crafted to fit you rather than reconstructed from a one-size-fits-all version.

The design process is cyclical, constantly balancing your dreams, resources, time, and budget. The final solution is somewhat of a moving target that evolves as one component influences another, until all of the pieces fit together in harmony.

## Steps to Success

The following outline provides important steps to follow in incorporating the design process into your project.

### Survey the Scene

Assess what you have, what is worth keeping, and what has to be changed. A good exercise is to list ten favorite qualities of where you live now alongside of ten least favorite. If you can't come up with anything positive about your current residence, think of another place that you enjoy and list the qualities of that location. Try not to get caught thinking that you must duplicate the status quo.

### Define Objectives of "Home"

Early phases of design call for an open-minded approach. Before delving into the idea of whether you would like a Southwest or Colonial-style home, you need to consider deeper issues. A fun and valuable exercise is to have those living in the house brainstorm ideas about "home" together. Using a flip chart and markers, jot down any notions about home that come to mind. These may include things such as "waste-free home," "grow all of our food," "dog needs a bath," "lots of light," and "keep cars away." It also may include "I want to sip my morning coffee in an outdoor room with a view" or "I'd like to curl up with a good book where no one will find me."

The following list of questions may help get your discussion started:

- What do we want to come home to?
- How can a home welcome and embrace us?
- How do we wish to interact with each other in our home?
- How can our home help us live in harmony with our values?
- How would we describe the perfect day in our home?

Because there is typically more than one individual living in a home, each person will have to answer these questions in his or her own way. A typical result of this process is that family members discover things about each other and themselves that they never knew. Your list will be unique, and possibly even humorous.

---

**General Design Considerations**

- What will it take to build it?
- What will it take to use it?
- How long will it last me? (in terms of style, function, timelessness, durability, and flexibility)
- Does it give me pleasure?
- Does it enhance my well-being?

## Think of Actions, Not Spaces

Think imaginatively about living in a new place. Rather than thinking of a home as linking boxes of space labeled "living room," "kitchen," and "bedroom," consider movement, activity, flow, and flexibility. Then organize spaces around this activity. All too often, kitchens are designed to showcase appliances. Little thought is given to human interaction other than the standard "triangle" work space. We look at where things will fit and try to get a sense of what looks like enough counter space. Yet in today's household, the kitchen has been transformed into a place of prominence and importance in family function. It is now not simply a place to store and prepare food but a place of conversation, cooperation, creativity, and sharing. We should embrace this new stature and give the kitchen area the design intention it deserves.

From there you may move on to more practical considerations. What does each function require for lighting, views, privacy, size, and warmth? You will then want to go through the desired qualities of each space and consider such details as what type and how much storage is required, what special furnishings or décor will be displayed, and so on.

## Tally Resources

Assess the resources of your site. These include natural, human, and information resources. For example, what are the natural features that drew you to the site in the first place? While it may be tempting to place your home in the most visually appealing place on the site, doing so may destroy the very quality that gave the site value. Consider ways that allow you to benefit from and enjoy those features. What natural resources may be tapped (solar access, wind patterns, building materials, water flows, soil stability and composition)? The more resources

D o I LIKE IT, DOES IT WORK, AND
CAN I AFFORD IT?"

—ARCHITECT WILLIAM MCDONOUGH

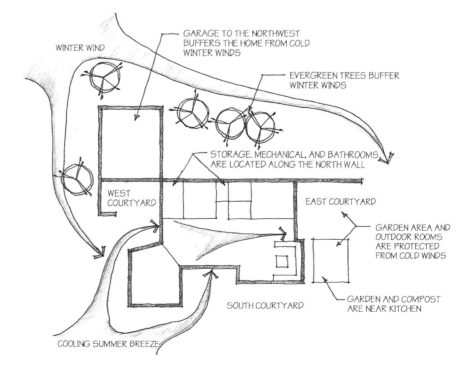

WINTER WIND

GARAGE TO THE NORTHWEST
BUFFERS THE HOME FROM COLD
WINTER WINDS

EVERGREEN TREES BUFFER
WINTER WINDS

STORAGE, MECHANICAL, AND BATHROOMS
ARE LOCATED ALONG THE NORTH WALL

WEST
COURTYARD

EAST COURTYARD

GARDEN AREA AND
OUTDOOR ROOMS
ARE PROTECTED
FROM COLD WINDS

SOUTH COURTYARD

GARDEN AND COMPOST
ARE NEAR KITCHEN

COOLING SUMMER BREEZE

we can utilize from the site, the less of an impact we will have on the greater environment. Sun, wind, and soil can provide energy for heating, cooling, and lighting. Water can provide cooling and purifying functions. The use of on-site materials will strengthen our sense of place without mining and transportation impacts of processed and shipped materials.

Next, consider daily living patterns in conjunction with solar patterns. We can predict movement through our homes based on our living patterns. You may wish to wake up and enjoy breakfast with the morning sun, utilize the living space or home office throughout the day, and dine with a sunset. I have experienced homes that considered views without regard to solar patterns with disastrous results to comfort and energy use. These homes, typically in a noncooling climate, created an expanse of west-facing glass that affected the occupants with uncomfortable heat gain (requiring air-conditioning) and severe glare (which impeded the appreciation for views they were trying to achieve). Supplemental less-frequented spaces such as utility, storage, and mechanical spaces require little interaction with the sun's movement and may be located in buffer zones on north or west sides. Living spaces extended to the outside consider natural breezes as well as solar exposure. Seasonal wind directions can be enhanced or blocked by the building form and landscaping. (See *sketch on opposite page*.)

Information gathering should be most intense at this phase but will continue throughout the design process. I encourage clients to do much of their research prior to selecting a design team. It is both useful and desirable to be prepared with a folder full of clippings from magazines or photos of spaces you enjoy. Whether it is the way the sunlight strikes a surface, the cozy feel of a room, or captured views, these images can help to inform the design of your unique home. Remember, design is an evolutionary process involving many ideas, knowledge bases, and experiences (see Resources section).

This is also the time to gather human resources. Your team may include an architect, contractor, and other professionals, as well as family and friends, with you as the captain. Once you have an idea of the scope and complexity (or simplicity) of your project, you will be able to define expertise and abilities needed to assist with your goals. There are several options before you. You will find services that range from a draftsperson to draw up your ideas, to design-build firms, to licensed architects that provide a partial or full service. Whatever method you select, it is important to bring your design team on board as early as possible (see Selecting a Team on page 33).

"WHY NOT GO OUT ON A LIMB—THAT'S WHERE THE FRUIT IS." —WILL ROGERS

## Making Research a Reality

The next step is turning your research into a three-dimensional, livable reality. Your design team works to translate your notes, images, and ideas of home into a technical document that will serve as the construction "how-to" manual. This may include site and landscape plans; floor plans; interior and exterior elevations; building sections and details; electrical and mechanical layouts; and structural plans, details, and calculations.

On residential-scale projects, it is typical for written specifications to be included on the drawings, and cover materials, methods, and procedures to be utilized. They may be as simple as a listing of manufacturer preferences with contact information. Useful specifications are especially important when building green. It should be clarified up front that the specifications were created as a tool to assist the contractor in meeting the project goals, not to hinder the process.

With computer-aided design, it is easy to explore options and variations to design schemes. It is much easier to move a wall on paper than during the construction process. It goes without saying that proper design and planning can actually save time and money in the long run by reducing the possibility of changes and unsolved issues in the field.

Design is best executed if it displays a clear vision. It follows that a good designer has the ability to understand and reflect that vision.

## Common Questions and Comments

I often hear the following questions and comments from clients regarding design. In addition to these, you will have questions of your own. Addressing these early on will enable a smoother design process.

### "What if I get tired of it?"

This is a comment I usually hear when a client is considering a daring move for his or her home, perhaps a color, or a new type of material. I wonder why they don't worry about getting tired of an off-the-shelf, typical solution. Is it because it is so bland that it becomes background static and not even noticed? While it is true that we do grow accustomed to our surroundings over time, boredom is not the inevitable result. We don't expect all of the people we know to act, dress, and behave the same way, nor would that be pleasurable. We find pleasure in character, discovery, and uniqueness. Why shouldn't our home express a unique character that we may grow accustomed to but also grow to appreciate and cherish?

### "I like it but I wouldn't want to live there."

Ask yourself why. You may have a very valid point, but it is a question worth asking and no one but you can answer it. Is the design a bit too quirky? Doesn't match your furniture? Your grandmother would think you're crazy? Perhaps those barriers are easier to face than you think, and there are aspects of the home that you would find quite livable.

### "It's not what I expected . . . but I like it."

You've been to dozens of home shows, looked through piles of plan books and magazines, and have determined what you'd really love is an English cottage. You walk into your architect's office and declare your desires. I have been across the drawing board on such a request, and while I love the character of an English cottage there is a time and place for it and there is a time and place for other solutions. In this case, I took the approach of presenting the requested solution as well as an "alternative" and received the above response. "It's not what I expected . . . but I like it" is my favorite comment by clients. You may be dead set on that English cottage concept and will find it easy to have one drawn up. I suggest however, that you enter your architect's office with open minds, eyes, and ears. You may very well come back to the idea of the cottage, but if you don't openly explore your options, you may have regrets down the road.

## Putting Sustainability into Design

The steps to creating good design provide means to efficient, healthy, and environmentally friendly homes. In other words, sustainable design and good design are one and the same. Green design is based on the notion that we can have positive impacts on nearby and distant human and eco-systems through thoughtful actions. It calls for living with natural systems rather than relying purely on technical support for our survival.

It can be a bit overwhelming for us to think of the scale of environmental problems we have to face. How can an individual really make a difference? Won't it take a revolution? I believe the revolution has begun. The beginnings are rooted in the empowerment of each of us making decisions for our own living. Starting within ourselves, our actions affect the place where we take root, our families, friends, community, and so on. There is a collective conscience about the need to live more sustainably—it's not just a few people on the fringe. Through research for this book, I have encountered a greater community of owners, builders, and designers that are working to improve how things are done. They are meeting the challenges of today's cultural, social, economic, and market influences that had been seen as barriers to building green. They are dissolving those barriers with powerful success stories.

## Selecting a Team

The following steps will help you select the right team for your project.

### What type of professional services do I need?

The answer to this question depends on several factors: the complexity of the project, your expectations, your knowledge about building systems, what professionals are available to you, your time, and your financial resources. In some cases, it may make the most sense to design and build your own home. While there are several benefits to this approach, it is not an attainable goal for most due to lack of skill or time. In most cases where you would like to do as much of the work yourself as possible, you should consider where your greatest challenges lie, then fill in those areas with professional help as needed.

● Architect/Contractor

The typical method today for building a custom home entails hiring an architect to design the home and a contractor to build it. There may be consultants to the architect such as structural, mechanical, and electrical engineers to provide specific detailed information. When the architect's drawings are complete, contractors are brought into the picture to bid (or provide cost estimates) for the project. A selection of a contractor is made and construction commences. Acting as the owner's representative, the architect oversees the construction process to ensure the design intention is being met. Once final completion is verified, you move into your home. Although this is the most typical arrangement, this linear method leaves out a valuable step—that of an integrated team approach. It is advisable to bring all parties into the process early on. Doing so has several benefits to you. First, it will ensure that all parties are knowledgeable about your goals and therefore stand a greater chance of meeting those goals. It also provides a greater chance of finding opportunities to maximize efficiencies within your home, and allows your team to set realistic budget and time schedules based on the design.

● Design/Build Firm

Another option is the use of a design-build firm. These are typically construction companies that also provide a design and drafting service. In this case much of your team is already on board and will work with you through all phases of the project. The drawback to this approach is that you may not have a trained designer available to you, possibly limiting some creative options. Another issue is the certainty of who will be looking out for your best interest. An architect works as the owner's agent in dealings with the contractor in order to keep your interest a priority. If the contractor leads the way, issues such as schedule and budget may supercede other goals.

● Owner-Builder

Owner-builder means that you will act as the general contractor by having your hands directly in the project, managing project sequencing and budget, and locating and working with subcontractors. This structure may be used for various reasons. With the overhead and profit of some contractors as much as 20%, owners may realize substantial financial savings by doing the work themselves. Realize however that there is a direct trade-off between time and money. Building a home is a full-time effort and a great deal of work. Time is also added through the learning curve. Professional construction firms come with years of experience and knowledge. Most homeowners do not have relationships with subcontracting trades, who tend to give priority to established construction firms that will bring them repeat business. Because sequencing of construction is so important, one subcontractor could create a great time setback.

Another reason people opt to use the owner-builder approach may simply be the desire to create their own space. Certainly, through history, we have spent more time as owner-builders than we have paying others to build our homes. Modern construction methods have added complications to the building process that have taken away individuals' confidence in their abilities. Fortunately, many green design concepts call for a simplified, more user- and builder-friendly approach. Systems such as straw bale, adobe, and straw clay empower individuals of all ages and abilities by allowing participation on various levels. If you are planning to be an owner-builder, your design decisions should aim at including builder-friendly green building methods.

## Can I Afford to Hire an Architect?

I believe that we all have a right to good design. In reality, we get what we can afford and choose to pay for. It seems that hiring an architect is often viewed as an extravagant expense, while we take for granted other prices of services accompanying a new home. Realtor fees, for instance, are typically in the range of 6% of the purchase of a home or land. Contractor fees range from 10 to 20% of the cost of construction. Their fees are rolled into the cost of building but are actually the overhead and profit added to the cost of materials and labor. Acceptance of realtor and contractor fees has to do with a perceived value. You can see tangible physical evidence of the purchase in the form of land or a building.

Architects provide a service, not a product. Placing a value on this service can be difficult for many to quantify. Architect's fees may range from 5 to 15% of the cost of construction, a fixed fee for a specified scope of services, or an hourly rate. Full architectural services will take you from initial site investigations through research, programming, design, drawings, and construction management of the project until move-in time.

## Phases of Architectural Services

● Pre-Design

This phase includes site analysis, zoning, and building code review, as well as programming to define design objectives and criteria.

● Schematic Design

Refinement of objectives and goals leads to a conceptual design. Relationships of space and basic building form are worked out in this phase.

● Design Development

The design is refined to produce drawings of floor plans, exterior building elevations, building sections, and any other critical building elements. Details and specific refinements of the design to meet owner's needs are resolved.

● Construction Documents

Detailed drawings of the building are made in 1/4-inch and larger scales. They include floor plans, building exterior elevations, building sections, wall sections, details, windows, doors, hardware, plumbing fixtures, and electrical fixture

schedules as required. The documents also contain mechanical, electrical, plumbing, and structural drawings, including footing and foundation plans, floor framing plans, and roof framing plans. Written specifications (detailing material and equipment selection), as well as building methods, accompany the drawings to complete the contract documents.

● Bidding and Negotiation

This phase assists the owner with contractor selection and negotiation of owner-contractor agreements. Clarifications or refinement of budget items in contract documents are made as required for bidding.

● Construction Administration

This phase includes observation of construction, verifying compliance with the drawings, answering questions regarding the drawings, solving unanticipated problems, and reviewing pay requests from the sub-contractors as needed.

## Finding the Right Help

There is an expanding awareness of sustainability among the general public, which has created the demand for a growing number of professionals specializing in green design and construction. Individuals making more environmentally conscious choices have greatly influenced how design offices function, as well as big industry that supplies the materials specified. Be aware, however, that not all green designers are created equal. *Greenwashing* is a term used to describe the deception by individuals or companies that tout invalid claims of green features. Greenwashing can occur at any level, from design to product selection. You may find a supposed green professional who has used a few recycled products and that is the extent of his or her expertise. Truly green design infiltrates all aspects of design—it is not an add-on option. It takes a keen awareness to make the distinction between greenwashing and valid claims. As with any business relationship, thoroughly check references and claims before making a commitment.

Architects can provide you with technical expertise and creative skills. They are licensed professionals with years of training, developing skills that range from the conceptual to the practical nuts and bolts of making buildings. The goal of a good architect is to integrate art, function, technology, and culture into buildings while maximizing health, safety, and comfort. Certainly in the most basic sense designers are responsible for the health, well-being, and enjoyment by their clients of their homes. It follows then that good design cannot be accomplished without addressing issues of sustainability.

Contractors provide skills that take your project from a paper dream to a physical reality. Their services typically include cost estimating, scheduling, coordinating trades, and communications with the architect. Most also provide a substantial amount of hands-on labor and, in some cases, specialties such as custom finish work..

Word of mouth is a great place to begin looking for an architect or contractor. Friends, family, and acquaintances often know someone with a successful building story. Next, you may want to check organizations that specialize in green construction in your area (see Resources section). Your architect or designer may have a list of several contractors they have had good working relations with. You should start with a list of at least three options that you will interview for the job. Since designing and building a home is so personal, you should interview these candidates face to face. Your selection should be based largely on your ability to communicate with them, and your level of trust in them, in addition to their work qualifications.

When forming your team you are acting as a matchmaker by creating a "marriage," in the business sense, between your contractor and architect. The happiness of this arrangement influences your satisfaction with the project. You may have found the perfect individuals to perform the work for you, however, if they can't communicate, your project will likely fall victim to less than ideal circumstances.

It may not be possible to locate an architect and builder well-versed in green design and construction in your area. This should not be a setback for you. Building green is more like refining one's speech than learning a new language. Strive to locate professionals experienced in innovative, open-minded design and who are excited and willing to explore possibilities with you. Let them know that you plan to participate in a give-and-take process of educating one another. Each party should be prepared to invest time in this learning process.

With all of the information available to designers and builders, there are few reasons for not providing the owner with a healthy, efficient, and durable home. This does not mean it will be accomplished without hurdles. Some challenges that may face your team include additional time invested in research and design, budget and schedule constraints, and an occasionally moving target of the owner's goals. There are trade-offs that need to occur in any project between cost, time, and quality. The prioritization of these elements is up to the owner to establish and the team to carry through.

## The Interview

Once you have defined your project's goals, you may more easily formulate a series of questions for your potential architect and contractor. Here are a few examples:

- Do you have experience meeting the types of goals outlined?
- What is your firm's philosophy?
- What additional expertise will you require for alternative building and energy systems?
- What is your specialty and how does it apply to my project?
- Are you willing to participate in regular meetings with the design and construction team throughout the stages of progress to ensure we are on target?
- How will you handle adjustments during design and construction that may be necessary based on new information?
- Do you have examples of similar work and references that may be contacted?

## Contracts/Agreements

Even professionals with the best intentions often get sidetracked by many issues that need to be addressed on a daily basis, from coordinating subcontractors and consultants to staying on budget and schedule. It is essential that the project team remain committed to the process and goals you have outlined. If you are concerned about this issue, the commitment may take the form of contractual agreements.

Contracts come in many shapes and sizes. As one client stated after reviewing a contractor's proposal, "Streets are named after contracts like this . . . One Way." Obviously, you want to avoid these types of contracts. While we all have to look after our own interests, contracts can and should be fair. Never sign something you don't understand! If the language that is used in the contract intimidates you, have it rewritten until you feel the intent is clear. The American Institute of Architects (AIA) has developed contracts for agreements between owners, architects, and contractors that can be purchased for a nominal fee. You may choose to use their documents directly or add modifications that suit your project. If you write your own or modify an existing contract, it is advisable to have this reviewed by an attorney prior to use.

## Construction Schedule

The contractor is key to expediting the building process. You and your architect should assist the contractor in becoming prepared and educated about green materials and systems before commencement of work. If the contractor is not in favor of building to your goals, he or she will likely slow the process through perceived barriers. If they are prepared and open-minded, you may build green faster than building conventionally.  ■

### Sample Contract Language

The following is an example of language that could be included in a contract to facilitate a smooth process with regard to building green.

**Contractor:**
Alternatives to those specified in the contract documents are to be approved in writing by the architect. Alternatives are to be proposed well in advance to eliminate possible delays in the project schedule. Alternatives not approved may be rejected at which time their removal and replacement will be the responsibility of the contractor with no penalty of time or expense to the owner.

**Architect:**
Architect shall specify materials and systems that are deemed to be healthy, efficient, durable, and appropriate to the scale and type of this project. Where means to meet this requirement are not available, the architect shall notify the owner with reason and possible alternatives for the owner's written acceptance.

## SUSTAINABLE FEATURES

- New Urbanist community
- Proximity to transit and services
- Small home design
- Passive solar
- Natural ventilation

# LUCAS-DAWSON HOUSE:
# Small Home Design

This home is located in the New Urbanist planned community of Prospect New Town in Longmont, Colorado. The planning concept of New Urbanism emerged in the early 1990s as a response to the poor design aspects of the post-war American suburb, with its unwelcoming garage-dominated fronts, homogenous styles, and auto-dependence. This alternative set out to provide new towns and developments with a sense of community common in early-twentieth-century towns, while responding to the needs of today's neighborhoods. In these communities, the dwellings, retail, entertainment, and recreation are commingled. Architectural styles encourage interaction and connection of people within their neighborhood.

### Site

Although this home incorporates many environmentally sensitive design features, its location is perhaps the greenest aspect of this home. The community houses a mix of architectural styles, housing types, mixed use commercial and public parks and amenities—most within a five-minute walk from any home. This arrangement allows resi-

**Location:** New Prospect Town, Longmont, Colorado
**Designers:** Terra Firma Inc.: Alisa Dworsky and Daniel Sagan, project team
**Owners:** Adam and Paula Dawson
**Square Footage:** 1,460
**Cost:** $100 per sq. ft.
**Builder:** Don Lucas
**Photographer:** Daniel Sagan

Photo © Ron Ruscio

LEFT

*The detached garage eliminates potential pollutants in the home for improved air quality. By placing the garage and home along the north property line, solar exposure is optimized.*

FACING

*Form and function create a fun dynamic as the home responds to the neighborhood context of this New Urbanist community.*

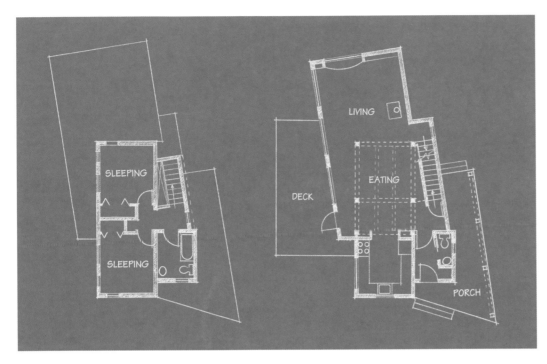

Don, because there was no heating system installed in the house yet. As construction neared completion, the house began to attract buyers. This was a pleasant surprise to Don, who now says, "As a spec builder I went out on a limb with this design, and I would have never imagined the positive responses I have received. I love the house; it's one of the best things I ever did."

The home's design incorporates the architect's strategy of small passive solar home designs. The compact nature means less land required to build, less material resources used, and less energy to operate. This design strategy is compatible with its urban setting, which typically provides smaller lots. With a busy road to the north, the home has few openings on that elevation. This works well with the spatial zoning and efficiency of the building shell. The house is placed on the north side of the lot to allow for solar gain into the windows and to create a usable yard in a pleasing part of the site.

The building form and room layouts are designed to enable the flow of warm air through the home. The southern elevation, containing the main living areas, is opened up to the sun with spaces such as stairs and bathrooms placed against the north wall. There is thermal mass in the floor of the living and dining room, which helps to store solar heat in the wintertime and facilitate cooling in the summer. In addition to passive solar heating, the house is organized to have one heat source on the main level. Since there are limitations on wood burning in Colorado, a gas stove serves as the single source heating plant. An exposed structure of

dents to live, work, and shop within their community—reducing transportation demands while strengthening neighborhood bonds. The mix of housing options allows families to respond to changes in size and housing need without leaving their community.

Prospect New Town is primarily being built by spec builders who develop one house lot at a time with unique designs. The town architect presented the design of this home to builder Don Lucas. Unfamiliar with any houses of this design, Don admits he was a little skeptical initially. As the construction progressed he became more enamored with the house.

### Energy

One cold November day, he called to announce that he and the electrician had entered the house to find that it was quite warm inside. This was interesting to

heavy timber and glue-laminated beams with 2-inch x 6-inch decking provides an aesthetic connection to the construction while conserving materials, such as dry-wall and finish woodwork, typically used to conceal the structure.

### Indoor Environmental Quality

In Colorado's dry summer climate, comfort is easily achieved with proper ventilation strategies. The ceiling fan facilitates cooling by blowing air across the concrete floor. The stairway acts as a passive ventilation passage in the summer as well as a plenum for heated air in the winter. Cross-ventilation is achieved with the thoughtful placement of operable windows to allow for easy passive ventilation of the whole structure.

The home was purchased by Paula and Adam Dawson, who have been very pleased with its functionality and performance. They say it is very easy to heat; they rarely use the central heating and they have not used the air-conditioning system since they moved in. The fact that the house is on a small urban lot, close to infrastructure, means that it uses less land. Being within walking distance to stores and restaurants gives the owners an added benefit and appreciation for their home.

More information about the New Urbanist planned community can be found on their website at www.prospectnewtown.com. ■

BELOW
*Exposed floor beams above the dining room reduce the amount of finish material used and create a detailed definition of the space with the warmth of natural wood.*

# LITTLE RESIDENCE:
# Design Intent

Just outside Santa Fe, a couple decides to escape the bustle of the city for a more intentional way of living that reflects their philosophy and life choices. As practitioners and teachers of yoga, their way of living revolves around health—spiritual, physical, and emotional. They choose organic food to nourish their bodies, and likewise wished to be surrounded by beneficial forms and materials. "We wanted our home to be a sanctuary—we wanted to feel nourished in a natural home, similar to the effect of a yoga posture," they explain.

The stylistic theme that drove the design of their home centered around their love of simple, natural things. They found expressions of this aesthetic in the design elements of Japan, where they had honeymooned. The Japanese strategy of connecting interior with the exterior both physically and visually was another important aspect they wanted to incorporate, and was well suited to the climate and location of their home.

They were inspired by the home of architect Paula Baker-Laporte, who practiced yoga with them. Paula also shared a similar philosophy of healthy simple living. Her specialty in designing smaller, efficient homes was right on target. These aspects made the process of working with Paula quite easy.

### Site
The single-story solution responds to the owners' desire to blend subtly into the landscape that is surrounded by

**Location:** Santa Fe, New Mexico
**Architect:** Baker-Laporte and Associates
**Owners:** Tias and Surya Little
**Square Footage:** 1,350
**Cost:** Not available
**Builder:** Robert Laporte
**Photographer:** Paula Baker-Laporte

## SUSTAINABLE FEATURES

- Preserved existing vegetation
- Rainwater catchment
- Sustainably harvested timber frame with straw clay wrap
- Natural earthen plastered walls inside and out
- Natural stone finishes
- Flexible functional space
- Compact size
- Highly insulated envelope
- Passive solar design
- Daylight and cross ventilation
- Energy-saving appliances
- EMF control
- Nontoxic finishes
- Breathable wall system

ABOVE
*A large roof overhang extends the living space to the outdoors and protects the exterior from wear. The strong horizontal lines reflect the terrain to anchor the home to the landscape.*

FACING
*The structural system of the timber framing defines the light-filled core of the home to provide a focal point of activity. Minimally furnished, this space is easily adapted for entertainment, conversation, and yoga practice.*

piñon juniper. The home is built around the existing trees to minimize disturbance of the natural environment. A rainwater catchment system with a 3,000-gallon cistern provides water for landscaping needs.

### Materials

Paula, along with husband and builder Robert Laporte, design and build "Econests." These are homes that incorporate goals of sustainability from the ground up. A unique aspect of these homes Is the utilization of straw-clay walls, which wrap timber frames. The choice of building a straw-clay home met the owners' goals of working with natural, native materials and the desire to visually blend into the landscape. Each of Paula and Robert's clients are required to attend a building workshop as part of the design process. In this way, the owners are given a thorough understanding of, and appreciation for, the decisions that make up their home. They also have fun in the process.

The straw-clay walls create a "breathable wall" system where vapor and moisture are regulated, providing for a healthier indoor climate. In this way the building envelope serves a purpose similar to layers of clothing. The concept of the home as a "third skin" regulating outside influences was important to the owners' notion of good health.

Materials used throughout the home are natural, healthy, and sensitive to the environment. The timber frame, which provides the structural strength, is constructed of sustainably harvested wood. The straw-clay walls, comprised of agricultural waste-straw coated with clay, are finished with earthen plaster inside and

RIGHT
*Clean lines and attention to detail permeate this home without the sacrifice of functionality.*

FAR RIGHT
*Energy and water-conserving fixtures and appliances meet the owners' aesthetic desires while using fewer resources.*

BELOW
*The new south facing "sun bump" offers sweeping views of the site while minimizing the amount of east and west facing glass. Winter sun enters the home and is absorbed by the slate floor to provide comfortable radiant heat.*

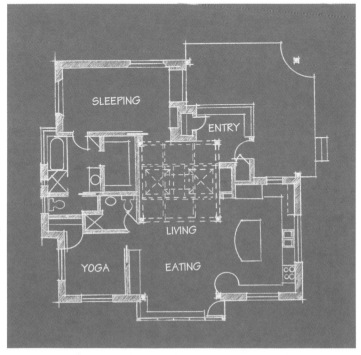

out. Natural stone finishes are used where durability of materials was needed, such as the entryway floor and kitchen countertops.

ABOVE

*The nature of materials is expressed in details such as the front entry support where stone meets wood in an elegant solution.*

## Construction

While some methods of natural building can pose challenges to building officials, the approval process for Econests is a smooth one. The architect and builder had assisted in developing a local code guideline for straw-clay, simplifying the permit process.

A thoroughly detailed set of specifications—the written instructions for the project—establish specific criteria for materials approved for use as well as recommended installation. These specifications act as a binding contract between the owners and the contractor to ensure that all aspects of the building meet the highest level of quality. It also serves as a guideline for subcontractors who may be unfamiliar with green building strategies.

The builder, Robert Laporte, finds great pleasure in the way the space is brought to life during the construction process. "It's a privilege to build something intelligent," he says. "It's magical, the way a thoughtful design can create what I call the fourth dimension—the 'feeling' of a space that gives pleasure."

Robert thinks that the success of the homes he builds is the result of time invested in good design. He says, "A home is only as good as the design." He has seen several occasions where Paula saved a client substantial money by meeting his or her goals with less square footage. Robert recalls one occasion when a client who wanted 2,000 square feet was given a tour of an Econest. Without knowing that the home was only 1,500 square feet, he declared the size was "just right" and proceeded to build a smaller home.

The owners had their hands, quite literally, in the construction of their home. They were involved with the selection as well as the application of the wall plasters, which provide a beautiful luminosity throughout the space.

### Space

The space and finishes in the home are conducive to performing yoga. The open floor plan and minimal furniture provide room for props and movement. Comfort is provided by a wood floor with radiant heat and passive solar, which is contained within a highly insulative building shell. Handcrafted shoji screens open and close easily to create flexible living spaces.

Clean lines, polished finishes, and careful attention to detail give this home a Zen-like quality. Every element is placed intentionally and with precision. Wide overhangs, wood detailing, and a rice paper ceiling illuminated from above connect the home further to Japanese influences. The "sun bump" offers views of the outdoors while the slate wood floor absorbs the warmth of the sun.

### Energy

From the foundation to the roof, the building envelope creates a thermally efficient barrier to the elements. Insulated concrete forms make up the foundation system, the straw-clay walls perform at an R-24, and the ceiling is super-insulated to an R-68.

Passive solar strategies were maximized. The building is oriented toward the sun with large overhangs that control the amount of heat gain. Interior mass materials provide thermal storage of solar gain for a more comfortable and efficient distribution of heat.

Windows that provide passive solar heating also bring ample daylight into the rooms, reducing the need for electric lighting during the day. The sizing and location of operable windows enhance cross ventilation through the home for comfort in the summertime.

Energy-saving and water-saving appliances and fixtures were installed, including an Asco dishwasher and a Vestfrost refrigerator.

### Indoor Environmental Quality

Specifications for materials in this home were based on the book *Prescriptions for a Healthy House*, that Paula coauthored with Lisa Flynn and John Banta. In it, she thoroughly details

ABOVE
*Niches carved out of the straw clay walls display special treasures that the owners have collected.*

FACING
*Shoji doors into the bedroom allow for privacy or openness, while the translucency allows light to be shared between spaces.*

the considerations for optimum indoor environmental quality. Some key aspects that are an integral part of her designs are the elimination of formaldehyde and VOC-emitting products, electromagnetic control, and the use of hygroscopic materials. Hygroscopicity, the ability for a material to absorb and release moisture, balances the humidity level within the home as well as the electro climate. Unfinished wood and natural plaster serve this purpose while also eliminating the need for finishes that may off-gas harmful vapors. Electro-magnetic fields (EMFs) are controlled in the home by placing all wiring in metal conduit, and with the additional precaution of electrical kill switches in the bedrooms, where the most time is spent. ■

# SMALL STRAW BALE HOUSE:
# Appropriate Technology

Through the owner's twenty years as a holistic healer, she has learned the importance of caring for our bodies and eating whole, organic, and natural unprocessed foods. Through her work, she became increasingly aware of the affect people's surroundings have on both their physical and emotional well-being. It was difficult to heal clients who resided in toxic houses. This discovery led her to develop the philosophy that if we are to be truly healthy, then we need to care for our mind, body, and spirit, as well as the home in which we live.

"I remember coming into a classroom that had been newly renovated. The smells of the glues, carpets, and wallboard were so strong I could not remain in the room. Everyone was breathing it into their bodies with the absolute trust

**Location:** North of Napa Valley, California
**Architects:** Pete Gang & Kelly Lerner
**Owner:** Linda Drew
**Square Footage:** 1,300 conditioned floor area
**Cost:** $288,000
**Builder:** Linda Drew and friends
**Photographer:** Craig Eve

LEFT
*The doors are painted in two
stages to mimic the rich
color of the local manzanita
branches.*

FACING
*Landscaping with edible
plants is compatible with the
natural and unprocessed
composition of this home. A
rooftop cupola brings light
into the core of the home
while also providing a path
for natural cooling breezes.*

that someone, somewhere, was overseeing their environment at all times to keep it healthy for them. Wrong!" Linda says.

When the opportunity came for Linda to realize her dream of a healthy home, she wanted it to reflect her beliefs as well as to be integrated with the land. Her ultimate goal was to create a nontoxic house that was environmentally friendly.

"While living in Tucson I attended every conference and workshop on natural building and living that I could find," Linda says. "There I walked into my first straw bale house and took a deep breath—ahhh—I was being 'house hugged!' I wanted that for myself! I saw straw bale as a way to express what I felt was the right way to live on the earth. I had come home. Straw bale housing was an outer expression of healthy, integrated living."

### Site

One approaches the site of the home on a dirt road that winds its way through groves of mature valley live oak, blue oak, gray pine, and

## SUSTAINABLE FEATURES

- Straw bale construction with earthen plasters
- Slate, bamboo, and recycled Douglas fir flooring
- Recycled and salvaged materials in construction and finish
- Off-the-grid renewable energy production
- Passive solar design

- Energy-efficient envelope
- Radiant heat
- EMF control with electrical wiring installation
- EMF control with elimination of structural steel
- Natural, nontoxic finishes
- Reuse of gray water for landscaping

ABOVE
*On cool summer evenings, the owner retreats to
this outdoor "bedroom" under a grass canopy.
Encompassed by sights, sounds, and smells of
the surrounding forest, this space becomes a
tranquil getaway just yards from home.*

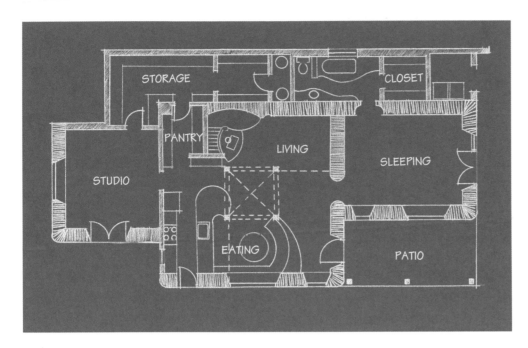

manzanita. Glimpses through the trees reveal a colorful haven nestled into a gently sloping hillside. Siting of the home considered preservation of the trees, as well as providing minimal visual disturbance of a nearby knoll. The orientation faces south and takes advantage of distant views while avoiding the power lines below. The climate is hot and dry, and summertime cooling is more of a concern than wintertime heating. The response is basic passive solar design to control the amount of sun and heat gain.

### Design

Building naturally can have its challenges in today's culture. Fortunately, Linda found architects Pete Gang and Kelly Lerner to help guide her through the process. They not only provided the design of the home but also worked with Linda throughout the entire process. In a sense, they served as facilitators in helping her create the house she wanted. They provided her with lists of recycled materials to research, taught her formulas for earthen plaster and paint making, and linked her with the right people to assist in

making the dream a reality. Finding natural materials that were less processed took great effort, focus, and tenacity. Many phone calls and trips to pick up materials in small, out-of-the-way places made for a huge learning curve every day.

Linda, along with many others, felt that the sharp right angles of conventional construction were not the proper way to house the human body. Straw bales are easily carved to soften edges and create niches.

While the house exceeded her original goal of 1,000 square feet, it is a comfortable size for one person without wasted space such as hallways. Spatial requirements varied from light to dark, high to low, cozy to open. The design has a three-part spatial organization—living room, studio, and bedroom.

"I had a high level of commitment to resource and energy-efficient design in a small house," Linda says.

### Construction

Linda served as the general contractor, overseeing workers, finding and collecting

materials, and constantly making decisions. She also provided manual labor. As a single woman with no previous building experience, she found the task stressful and difficult at times. Her house is proof, however, that with determination and a big learning curve, wonderful things are possible.

A commonly used strategy for people such as Linda is hosting building workshops. These workshops teach hands-on, natural building arts in exchange for labor. While hosting workshops helped get her house built and made that part of the project easy and fun, she acknowledges the difficulty of having to constantly train new people throughout the process, as "students" moved on. Still, the benefits of such help cannot be overstated. Twenty-five people raised the straw bale walls in two days, and two workshops on earthen plaster nearly completed the exterior walls in two weekends.

As a painter, potter, and writer, Linda needs space to create and display. The two-foot thick straw bale walls were accommodating. She carved out niches for art supplies and a long, vertical niche with shelves to display her teapots.

"My happiest day of construction was the day I applied the ornamentation with a fellow artist, Bernard. I created the Art Nouveau design and stippled it directly onto the wet plaster, then, using a potter's technique, applied fine mud plaster in small amounts to create the design above the dining area."

### Materials

The vivid wall colors throughout the house are all natural and handmade. The yellow kitchen wall is a natural caseine paint made from milk powder, lime, and natural yellow oxide pigment. The bedroom is blue alise, made from finely ground rock color pigments. While the alise paint was wet, Linda frescoed color by hand, rubbing additional pigments over the top to create more dimension.

The straw bales used for the walls were found forty miles away and are finished with plasters that utilize soil directly from the home's site.

Everywhere you look, the materials in the home tell a story of thoughtful selection and resourcefulness. Sustainably harvested maple counters and salvaged wood flooring add warmth to the kitchen. The timbers, both interior and exterior, were salvaged from various sources, including an old army barracks. Linda's collection of antique tiles was pressed into the wet plaster in distinctive spots. Reed mat ceilings provide a natural alternative to drywall, which is more energy-intensive to produce.

Material use is maximized by exposing the loft floor, salvaged from an Oakland army base, as the finished ceiling below. The posts and beams are 8-inch x 8-Inch Douglas fir posts from a McDonald Douglas factory in Los Angeles. Floor joists were salvaged from a Windsor, California, winery. The doorknobs were found at a local church's Christmas bazaar.

### Energy

Although this house sits just 200 feet from a public utility line, the owner chose energy independence with the installation of a photovoltaic (PV) system. The system consists of 16 photovoltaic solar collectors, a DC/AC inverter, and battery storage that are located a short distance from the residence in a small protective structure. Water is supplied by a well with a submersible pump powered by the PV system.

"I am off the grid, and do not have conveniences we assume are necessary: air-conditioning, garbage disposal, dishwasher, microwave. I do not miss any of them," Linda says.

Assuming responsibility for her energy brought the finer details of energy consumption to the forefront. After determining which uses are "must have" came the selection of the most efficient appliances. The refrigerator is a Sun Frost, which uses 20 percent less than a typical energy-efficient model. This has a substantial impact on energy use, considering refrigerators operate twenty-four hours a day.

Natural ventilation is provided by a cooling tower in the center of the home, which is surrounded by operable windows that draw out hot air during the summer. It also brings daylight into the core of the home while adding an interesting design element to the interior space and exterior style.

The straw bales provide highly insulated external walls with cellulose insulation in the roof and uniformly distributed thermal mass in the form of earthen plaster walls and slate floors. The result is an inside temperature of 70 degrees during winter when the sun shines. Additional heating is provided by a centrally located wood stove and in-floor radiant heat.

### Indoor Environmental Quality

There is no off-gassing to smell. Linda claims that the house is so natural that it could be eaten, but admits that the steel bolts in the wood structure may not go down so easily. The straw bales provide absolute soundproofing. Sounds don't carry from room to room and certainly not from the outside in. The walls have texture that is pleasing to the touch and the rounded edges soothe the body.

Linda has created a home that she feels expresses her personal beliefs about living for a healthy self as well as a healthy environment. She is happy to share it with visitors who, she hopes, will "become relaxed and happy, restored by the healing vibes of being house hugged." ∎

BELOW

*As an artist, the owner took advantage of the sculptural qualities of straw bale construction to build niches for displaying her work.*

# DWORSKY-SAGAN HOUSE:
# Flexibility

**Location:** Turnbridge, Vermont
**Designers**: Alisa Dworsky and Daniel Sagan
**Owners:** Alisa Dworsky and Daniel Sagan
**Square Footage:** 2,300
**Cost:** $110 per square foot
**Builder:** Alisa Dworsky and Daniel Sagan
**Photographer:** Daniel Sagan

The design of this house was created in response to concerns for flexibility, cost, energy efficiency, and the beauty of the site. Today the structure serves as both residence and workspace. As the family grows, the workspaces will move to a new structure; the studio is transformed into more bedrooms, and the workshop becomes a large living room.

"We chose to make the living spaces small. This is a result of our concern for our environment. Smaller houses not only use fewer resources for construction, but they use less energy for heating and cooling over the life of the building," say the owners. The added benefit is a reduction in construction, heating, and maintenance costs. Spaces were made gracious by raising ceiling heights to nine and ten feet. Each room receives plenty of natural light and views; most also include built-in storage.

### Site

"The siting of the house, the massing, and the details of the building envelope were largely determined by our desire to build an energy-efficient and climatically specific structure," the owners explain.

ABOVE
*The siting and verticality of this home are responses to the steeply sloping terrain as well as a desire to preserve large existing trees. Conifer trees to the north protect the home from cold winter winds. Deciduous trees to the south allow ample winter sun while shading during the summer.*

FACING
*Recycled steel siding and roofing, locally mined slate, and painted wood siding on a rainscreen provide a durable, low maintenance exterior.*

## SUSTAINABLE FEATURES

- Site responsive design
- Use of recycled materials
- Use of durable materials
- Use of local materials
- Passive solar design
- Super-insulated and draft free
- Constant flow of fresh air with heat recovery

The house's verticality is a response to the steeply sloping terrain. This minimized the amount of soil disturbance and allowed the owners to save many of the existing trees. The building is sited to take advantage of the southern exposure and views to the south and west. Because of its east-west orientation, each living space in the house has windows to the south, providing year-round daylight and solar heat gain in the winter. Less occupied spaces, such as the bathrooms and storage rooms, are located along the north wall. There is a grove of conifers to the north, which mitigates the winter winds. To the south are deciduous trees, which provide shade in summer while allowing direct sunshine to enter the house in winter.

## Materials

The primary construction material is wood and engineered lumber consisting of TJI joists, parrallams, microllams, and trusses. Each of these materials uses wood fiber more efficiently than dimensional lumber, thus reducing the amount of trees used in construction. The exterior is made of painted wood on a breathing rain screen, recycled steel siding, and locally mined slate. The rain screen and the slate increase durability, and each siding choice was inspired by local building methods. The rain screen is an appropriate detail in this moist climate and is accomplished by creating a 3/4-inch air space between the structure and siding. While it adds some labor and material

ABOVE

*Living spaces are arranged to take advantage of warm air rising from the wood stove. During the summer months, cooling breezes move through the home and are exhausted above.*

to the installation, the siding lasts longer, making it a wise choice for the long term. The roof is finished with standing seam metal, which is a locally available craft and quite durable.

## Energy

The living spaces are oriented vertically to take advantage of warm air rising from the wood stove located on the lower level. This

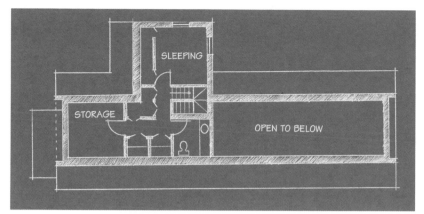

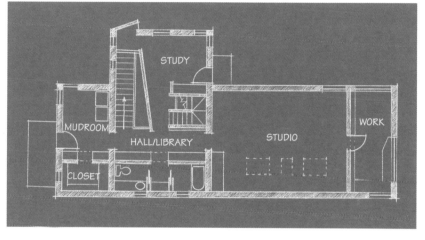

also helps to naturally cool and ventilate the house in the summer. The cooling strategy in Vermont is to keep the air moving through the stack effect and cross-ventilation. In Vermont the sun is low in the sky because of the state's high latitude, so the trees to the south are quite useful for shading.

The house is zoned, mechanically, into three separate areas. The main room downstairs and the two bedrooms upstairs are on separate zones. The workspaces, occupied only part of the day, operate on the third zone to avoid being fully heated for twenty-four hours. When the stove is in use or when it is sunny, the mechanical system does not operate. On sunny winter days, the house gains heat and remains comfortably above 70 degrees without the use of the wood stove or the boiler.

The building incorporates draft-free construction details. Superior air sealing was accomplished by using a polyethylene barrier from under the slab to the roof. This necessitated wrapping the barrier through the floor structure. While it created a tight envelope, it also created some complication for the construction process. In order to maintain the indoor air quality, fresh air enters the building through a heat-recovery ventilation system in which outside air is warmed from heat transferred from

the exhaust air leaving the building. The wood-framed building is insulated to an R-30, a level that is three times that required by local codes. The windows are highly energy-efficient models. Annual heating and hot-water costs are approximately $950 a year using 1½ cords of wood and the balance in propane, which serves a high-efficiency boiler. "We did not know if such a small stove would heat the house efficiently. We are extremely pleased with the home's performance thermally," the owners say.

### Design

Because the owners are also architects, they took many liberties to experiment with ideas that they may not have otherwise tried on clients' projects. Some of these ideas worked well while others did not, providing them with experience and the tools to introduce the successes into other projects.

They had experimented with adding a lot of built-in storage and making the rooms as small as possible. While the living room may have ended up two feet too narrow, the design

of a five-foot-wide hallway with bookshelves, replacing the need for a library room, functions quite well. They also left the first floor structure exposed to save cost and resources of having to add finish material. The hard surfaces have not created a sound transmission problem and the owners are happy with the appearance. With the forethought in planning for future changes, the home should suit the owners' needs for many years to come. ■

# CHAPTER 3

# Design Strategies

With your goals more clearly defined you are better able to examine specific means to achieve those goals. Along with the basic tenets of sustainability there are also ways we can live more sustainably and enjoyably in our home by implementing specific design strategies. The following examples range from where you live to sorting through "stuff." These suggestions may or may not fit a particular circumstance, so feel free to "take them or leave them."

## Sense of Community with Neighbors

Where we live is as important as how we live, with regards to sustainable life-styles. The location of our home determines the community we are part of. This community may fit our life-style or require a modification of usual habits. If functioning properly, a community may strengthen ties with place, family, and friends; it may offer options for meeting needs and desires and allow us to live more intentional life-styles. For many, young and old included, access to services such as schools, shops, work, hospitals, and recreation within walking distance or alternative transit is an important asset. On the other hand, a community may malfunction by limiting our access and connections to others, discouraging a more environmentally friendly life-style, and creating a feeling of isolation. A case in point is the problem with many new suburban towns sprouting up across our nation. One often has to drive miles to purchase a gallon of milk, get to work and school, and recreate. This dependence on cars has more implications than the obvious resource depletion and pollution. It also reduces the amount of time we have for ourselves and loved ones, and eliminates opportunities for positive social interactions.

Establishing a sense of community will foster a connectedness to place. Once connected, we are more committed to solving problems and improving imperfections. If we are in a constant state of transition from one community to another, we may not take responsibility for it and leave problems for others to solve. Individuals and communities shape one another over time. When my husband and I moved into our home, we had only intended to stay for five years. Without much thought, we began making changes that reflected our lifestyle, needs, and tastes. We began to nest and settle into place to a point of comfort. Ten years later, while we are still not living in our dream home, we have fallen in love with our neighborhood as well as the comfort that our home brings. Now when my three-year-old says, "I want to go home" after a long day, I feel a great sense of pride.

Not to be forgotten in the discussion of community are the people that comprise it. This is an asset not accounted for on real estate appraisals, but it may be the most valuable. Cooperation among neighbors, whether five yards or five miles away, can greatly improve the quality of life for all involved. Our neighborhood shares carpools, child and pet supervision, meals, milk delivery service, and an occasional bottle of wine on the front porch. This country has a rich history of cooperative living that dates back to 700 A.D. with the Native American

Photo © Kraus-Fitch Architects

ABOVE

*At Pioneer Valley Cohousing in Amherst, Massachusetts, the common house provides a place for residents to enjoy conversation, share a meal, or read a book from the common library as children play in the courtyard.*

F IND YOUR PLACE ON THE
PLANET, DIG IN, AND TAKE
RESPONSIBILITY FROM THERE."

—GARY SNYDER

culture. In more recent times, the European settlers found cooperation among neighbors essential to their survival. Today this cooperation has evolved into what we call "division of labor." This terminology, however, is derived from our experience of segregating tasks rather than integrating them. This not-so-subtle distinction means that we have moved from a culture of cooperation to one of competition, which has become evident in the designs of homes, towns, and cities.

While many families and communities have managed to maintain the positive aspects of cooperation, it has become less of a norm. Urban sprawl has served to connect people to their automobiles more than to their neighbors. In opposition to this movement, a cooperative nature of living reemerged in the early 1970s in Denmark. Intentionally planned neighborhoods, called cohousing, were developed. The idea centers around social support and cooperativeness among various families who maintain private residences with access to common facilities. Often these families are of varying structures ranging from singles to families with children, from the young to the elderly. Cohousing is based on the theory that we each have something to contribute to the greater community and that we may thrive with the support of others. The typical boundaries that separate individuals in a community are blurred as the residents share meals, skills, chores, and resources.

Cohousing developments provide ample opportunity for green design strategies. Affordability is an initial aspect that appeals to many who otherwise may not be able to afford a home of their own. This is accomplished not through lack of quality, but through sharing resources, building smaller, and using economies of scale. The cost of building and maintaining infrequently used spaces such as guest rooms, large eating areas, or exercise spaces can be shared by the entire group. Individual kitchens, for instance, can be reasonably sized for daily use with the common house sized and equipped to handle special gatherings. These shared spaces allow each individual unit to be sized appropriately, which also has a tremendous cost, resource, and energy savings. It is often more cost-effective to buy materials such as sustainably harvested lumber in bulk. Shared walls between units can substantially cut down on the amount of materials needed. Operation of these units are cost-efficient; designs incorporate strategies such as energy-efficient envelopes and centralized heating, cooling, and hot water systems. Renewable energy systems are often more feasible in greater scale than they would be for individual homes. These aspects provide a higher standard of living while also addressing affordability.

Site development is another unique aspect of cohousing. The typical strategy of clustered development preserves open space in its natural state, or for recreation and gardening. Vehicles are relegated to the periphery of the housing development, reducing noxious automobile fumes in living areas and leaving open internal space for personal interaction. This usually means safe play areas for children in the center of activity where adult supervision is easy.

Depending on the number of households and demographics of residents, there may be a need for basic services on site. By providing office space and shared equipment, exercise facilities, the use of food co-ops, and other services, the need for a daily vehicle trip may be eliminated for many.

## Communal Space for the Family

It is well understood that the design of our homes can send a message to visitors that is either welcoming or unwelcoming. Many new housing developments have homes that replace the front porch, where social interaction used to happen, with garages. This sends the message that "this is a place where cars live, not humans." Principles of community design that encourage interaction can be applied to influence interaction at the family level. The "family" room was an evolution in housing that responded to the needs of children, giving them space to play while still within the safety of their own homes. Placement and quality of this space can greatly influence the "family" aspect of this room. Who hasn't experienced the basement room stocked with television, computer, and video games with little natural light? Rather than being a place for family interaction it often becomes a hideout for the kids. This may be an appropriate solution in some cases. The point is to understand the social results of your design decisions. If family interaction is desired, place the room in which you want the family to gather in a desirable location.

## Appropriate Technology

If there's one thing that we can count on in this world, it is that the sun will rise tomorrow. Wind blows, water flows, and the earth maintains a constant temperature. If we rely on these forces of nature then it goes without saying that we have the ability to create a renewable and reliable source of energy. Has your home ever lost power in a storm? While it is refreshing to realize that we can survive without the flow of electricity, it's not an experience we want to live with for long. Energy independence means you can take control of where your energy comes from rather than depending on a utility company.

Renewable energy systems that utilize the sun, wind, water, and earth provide a service while offsetting initial costs of installation. A life-cycle costs analysis for renewable energy systems includes the payback period, which is the amount of time until the system pays for itself with the energy it produces. This method uses the current cost of energy for calculation purposes. In some cases, the analysis reveals a payback period of several years, which creates such responses as "I'll do it when it becomes competitive." The problem with such a formula is the fact that utility prices are not fixed and are dependent on a number of factors outside your control. As our nonrenewable sources diminish and demand increases, prices will respond, making for a much shorter payback period for renewables. Renewable energy allows you to take advantage of an investment today while providing a level of financial security in the future.

Depending on the location of your site, initial installation of renewable energy systems may be cost competitive with standard grid connection. If utilities need to be run a great distance, the cost may exceed that of a renewable system. Take this into consideration when selecting a site. Often a piece of property will be sold at a reduced rate due to a lack of utility service on the property. A portion of this savings can then be used to provide off-the-grid services. This allows you access to a piece of property that may be more appealing while encouraging you to be energy independent.

Perceived value has an impact on decisions as well. Renewable energy systems are often held to a standard above many other investments and purchases. What is the payback for the last car,

### Casualties of Convenience

American culture has created a deadly combination with regard to energy use. We have become dependent on energy supplies from limited nonrenewable sources, causing pollution and environmental degradation while simultaneously misusing this energy in meaningless ways. Is it worth these costs to operate an electric shaver, light an unoccupied room, or maintain clocks on appliances and that flashing "12:00" on the VCR? Appropriate technology recognizes the need for comfort and convenience without the wasteful by-products of clumsy design.

computer, or television you purchased? Their value will decrease over time. In fact, most technology-based equipment depreciates the minute you purchase it. A renewable energy system, however, gains value over time by saving money otherwise paid to a utility company. We tend to be drawn to the latest technologies even though last year's model was more than adequate at the time. In fact, it is likely that the typical consumer would purchase a number of cars and computers during the life of a photovoltaic system, which has a lifespan of thirty years or more.

Photo © Carolyn Bates

## Comfort

There's no use in discussing building design without consideration of user comfort and satisfaction. By using passive and efficient mechanical strategies, space can be controlled to provide the right temperature, humidity, and airflow. Beyond that, however, is the true realm of great design. As Santa Fe builder Robert Laporte states, "We need to also consider the fourth dimension of space—how it feels." This feeling is often hard to quantify, but it is experienced deeply. Words such as cozy, embracing, calm, pure, or uplifting are a good start. Can you remember a place where you just felt a sense of the space touching a chord within you? Think of the size, colors, lighting, textures, and décor. Within that space were there places that drew you in even further, such as a comfortable place to sit? If given the chance to nestle in, it was probably a little difficult to tear yourself away when the time came to leave. In our busy lifestyles, full of movement from one place to another, it is a treasure to experience a place that calls you to pause and enjoy.

ABOVE

*This eating area within a kitchen provides a place for personal interaction in the heart of activity. The window seat allows one to connect with others or to sit alone quietly enjoying the warm sunlight.*

## Rejuvenation

Sustainable design is not only about buildings that will sustain, but also about the means of sustaining the people who dwell within. Where do you go to think, dream, tinker, rest, and rejuvenate? We all have the need for different activities in our lives, which may have specific spatial requirements. When we are rested and balanced we are able to find a clearness of vision and purpose. This enables us to continue to live within our beliefs when times become challenging. This does not have to occur in a far away place, but can be a vacation within our homes. Sacred spaces can take many shapes and sizes, indoors or out.

I find that many male clients desire a workshop for this purpose. My theory is that this desire comes from the human need (or instinct) to create a means of living—to sustain their family with the work of their own hands. In one instance, where the owner had built the home himself, he no longer felt the need for the workshop and redesignated the space for exercise. Fortunately, the size and location were compatible for this new use.

## Size

Building size has great implications on the environment, your budget, and the usefulness and enjoyment of your home. Less space means fewer resources required to build, operate, and maintain your home. A square foot of space removed will eliminate a measurable amount of foundation, floor, wall, roof, electrical materials, and finishes, as well as volume of space to heat and cool. Ultimately this translates into your home costing "x" dollars a square foot; a home with less square feet provides an opportunity for substantial cost savings, not to mention resource savings. In addition to these practical matters, building smaller may actually provide you with a more enjoyable space.

While some may purchase vehicles based on size alone, most make their decision based on comfort, functionality, and style. As it relates to housing, that "bigger is better" philosophy has been a myth perpetuated by developers who can build more space cheaply and market it as an added benefit. Certainly we require space for the activities in our homes, however much of the space added to today's homes provides no added benefit for use or enjoyment. It simply adds to the "trophy status."

The soaring spaces of medieval cathedrals were designed to create a sense of awe by making the individual feel insignificant in the realm of the holy. Is this what you should be aiming for in a home? While cathedral ceilings may impress a visitor upon first glance, you're the one who has to live with them. Is the space comfortable and nurturing, or does it feel empty?

We must acknowledge the human scale when planning the spaces that enclose us. Most of us are between five and seven feet tall. While twenty-foot high ceilings may be appropriate in a museum or assembly room, they are not necessarily appropriate for everyday living. If you really want something special, why not invest in a detail, close to your touch, that you can interact with on a more intimate level than space alone can provide?

## Ease of Movement and Function

If it's not easy, it's probably not going to happen. Movement through our homes and between tasks is required on a daily basis and is simple enough to predict. Based on these predictions, we can make a functional pattern for design. Take, for instance, the kitchen. If you are composting daily waste, yet the compost pile is at the opposite end of your property, it may be a struggle to utilize. Why not locate this function close to its source and make your life easier? Taken a step further, since the garden is a regular user of the compost, it follows that the two should be in close proximity. To close the loop, it is also sensible to locate a garden near the kitchen since that is where the crop will be used. You can begin to see how one single function has a chain effect that influences design and placement of spaces in and around your home.

The idea of ease of movement and function also impacts your ability to live sustainably in your home. Some important tasks that require prior space planning and design include com-

WE ARE CREATURES OF RHYTHMS AND CYCLES. WHENEVER WE BEHAVE IN A WAY WHICH IS NOT IN TUNE WITH OUR NATURAL RHYTHMS AND CYCLES, WE RUN A VERY GOOD CHANCE OF DISTURBING OUR NATURAL PHYSIOLOGICAL AND EMOTIONAL FUNCTIONING." —CHRISTOPHER ALEXANDER, FROM *A PATTERN LANGUAGE*

posting (as just mentioned), recycling, storage for reusable items, proper food storage (to reduce waste from rot), convenient lighting controls and layout, space for air drying clothes, and bicycle storage, to name a few.

## Light

Regardless of where you build your home, the sun will be an issue you should address. You may shun or welcome it depending on the climate, time of year, and your own comfort requirements. Fortunately, we have the ability to precisely locate the sun in the sky throughout each hour of each day, making a comfortable relationship with the sun an achievable goal.

Solar responsive design is the most easily accomplished goal in building sustainable homes and has the least cost impact. Because our homes require windows for light, ventilation, views, and even potential exits, the cost of these openings is built into the budget for design.

If solar control is not handled properly, it may have a variety of negative effects. I have had clients who experienced extreme glare conditions in their existing homes, making them hesitant to work with the sun when designing new residences. Some homes located in cold, mountainous regions require air-conditioning due to the overheating from solar gain. Too much glazing will also create a heat loss problem, since most glass rates at about R-4 for insulation levels. No one wants to sit by a cold and drafty wall, even if the view is spectacular. It is easy to spot homes with this design flaw; they have expansive glass walls facing views, yet consistently have the shades drawn. A wall of glass may look like a good solution on paper, but if handled improperly results in nothing more than an expensive frame for drapes.

Not to be understated is the emotional connection we have to natural light. Beauty can be found in the simplest expressions. For example, our home can capture light in a way that is reminiscent of the inviting light filtered through the leaves of a tree on a warm summer day.

## Beauty of Nature

Sensuous, comforting, embracing. Are these terms that describe your home? For many who have built using natural methods and materials, these terms are part of their everyday experience. Our bodies are not made of right angles. Why should we try to force them into boxes? Organic styles are easily created with many natural building methods and provide a soft enclosure that "embraces" rather than "contains" us.

Wabi-sabi is a design methodology based on the notion that from nature's irregularity and circumstance comes beauty. The imperfections in life are appreciated rather than scorned. A torn piece of cloth, a worn-in stone threshold, a piece of twisted driftwood—all are cherished items that carry a rich history. This natural expression is difficult to achieve with heavily processed materials. Such materials are not intended to wear and, when they do, fail to perform as they were intended. Natural materials, on the other hand, are of the earth and will return to the earth to repeat the cycle. As with people, character in materials is gained over time and their wear tells a rich and valuable story.

## Detailing

In green building design, we find ways to express ourselves through the crafting of space. It is an opportunity to display the treasures and qualities we hold dear. Detailing means more than decoration of a structure. There are opportunities to express ourselves in the colors and textures we choose, the way in which we assemble materials and components, and

### Distressed Materials

I find irony and humor with the current fashion of distressed materials. These are usually processed materials that have been treated in a manner that is supposed to show a life of use and reveal more of their natural state. Such a look is applied to wood timber structures and details, furnishings, and faux wall finishes through various painting techniques. There is quite a bit of effort (and energy) to achieve a quality that can be found easily by simply using natural materials, honestly. The trend however does show that our culture is finding value in natural colors, textures, and characteristics. We just need to learn how to achieve them honestly.

"To live more simply is to live more purposefully and with a minimum of needless distraction." —Duane Elgin

other aspects of composing our three-dimensional space.

My then-to-be husband and I were planning a sizable addition to our home as we approached our wedding day. While our friends deemed this crazy, the timing created a fortuitous circumstance. Since the building design coincided with wedding events, I was able to make a connection between the two through a design response that we appreciate every day. Two small spaces, carved out of the height of the vaulted ceiling, create a private "meditation" space in the sitting room and a light/view shelf in the master bedroom, which can only be accessed by a ladder. With the help of a friend and neighbor woodworker, we designed canopy poles to be used for the outdoor ceremony that could later be crafted into ladders. The ladders mimic the kiva ladders leading to sacred places we'd visited at Anasazi ruins and remind us of our wedding day. Green aspects are part of the equation as well. The sitting room loft is stepped back from the south façade, allowing daylight to penetrate the core of our home. The high placement of operable windows allows for airflow and ventilation control through our home. Children are always drawn to this space, finding it an adventure waiting to happen. The views of the city, mountains, and the large trees in the yard give us a greater connection to place and nature.

## Simplicity

Simplicity is not about sacrifice; it is about a commitment of doing more with less. Simplicity impacts design by creating spaces that enclose only the necessary and desirable aspects of our lives. Do we really need a room dedicated to knickknacks we can't touch and furniture we can't kick our feet up on?

The act of simplifying should be an empowering experience and may extend beyond stuff to include the people and places we interact with, the type of work we do, or the type of food we consume. By combating the stuff that clutters our homes and minds we will simplify our daily experience, leaving room for more meaningful thought processes and experiences.

## Stuff

Storage rooms are an evolution of days gone by when they housed essential items to our daily routine, such as items for food preparation. Today these rooms hold items that we may not interact with for years, if ever. Why are we storing them? How do we distinguish what is a keeper? To answer these questions we must ask ourselves what, why, and how we are storing.

### What

I am not suggesting that you strip away your family heirlooms and discard the photo albums. As you make a list of the items stored, you may find some valuable items worth storing and others that you have an immediate use for. In many cases, storage spaces are full of items that could be put to good use by someone other than you. If you have a use for them, why are they in storage? This is an excellent opportunity for reuse by either donating the items or by offsetting another's need to purchase new what they could find in your yard sale.

## Why

Consider the difference between clutter and cherished items. I encourage you to make a thoughtful examination of your things in order to determine what is meaningful and what is just clutter. People make professions out of clearing other people's clutter. It is a difficult thing to do on your own. There may be sentimental reasons you want to keep something, or you may simply have the thought "I might need that scrap of wood some day." If you are in fact one who does occasionally need a scrap of wood and will find it handy in the near future, then a little resourcefulness is a positive thing. If you are like most people however, those incidental items pile up over the years to create a mound of materials that not only take up physical space but mental space as well.

## How

Measure the storage space you now have, both in square feet and volume, to determine the cost of storing such items (in the form of building, heating, and cooling) and to look for ways to maximize the capacity of storage spaces. It is much more efficient to invest in shelving and organizers than in additional square feet. Rather than creating a storage "room," look for opportunities in the incidental nooks and crannies of your home that would otherwise go unused: space beneath a stair, built-in shelves along a hallway, bench seats in window nooks, accessible attic spaces, or even spaces within the depth of a wall.

## Outdoor Rooms

Outdoor rooms offer many benefits. They provide a place to enjoy nature through a physical connection to the outdoors, offer flexible living space which often can be utilized throughout the year, and extend the usable space of your home without the expense of a formal enclosure. Outdoor rooms should be easily accessible from major living areas if you plan on frequent use. Spaces with circulation through them, such as an entry courtyard, encourage use more than dead-end space. As with your home's interior spaces, design aspects such as thermal comfort, appropriate scale, lighting, and function should be considered. Outdoor rooms may be enclosed by partial walls and a roof or by a small gesture of strategically placed vegetation. Your property was the first investment and design decision for your home. Outdoor rooms help maximize enjoyment of its finer qualities.

In order for outdoor rooms to function through most of the year, you must first have an understanding of the natural forces of your site. Considerations for solar exposure and seasonal wind patterns will inform design responses to keep you protected and comfortable. While buildings draw a distinct boundary between inside and outside, we can find opportunities to blur that boundary in order to create a greater connection to the natural world.

## Flexibility

Family dynamics and size are continuously changing, sometimes by surprise. How can we properly plan for the unknown with our home's design?

With two young children, I am keenly aware of the need for family space that allows for common tasks of cooking, paying bills, relaxing, and entertaining all within reach and supervision of the youngsters. This family structure calls for a relatively open yet compact plan to keep sights and sounds nearby. What happens in twelve or so years when the emerging adolescent prefers loud music, private phone conversations, and sleeping until noon? Can the nursery become the home office? The guest room become the teenager's room?

Many of the addition projects I have designed involve homes where a family was raised and the kids have since left. Mom and Dad can now afford that extra space they've always dreamed of—a large family room, more closet space, and a functional kitchen to accommodate grandchildren's visits. But what if our homes were designed with the anticipation of such changing events. After all, it's not entirely a surprise that kids grow up and leave the nest and often bring young ones back to visit grandma and grandpa.

Flexibility can be addressed as simply as moving functions in existing spaces. In this case it is important to consider the size and placement of rooms relative to these changing functions. For instance, a home office that is placed away from the home's main activities may make for a private guest space in the future. Planning in this way will reduce the amount of time, materials, and cost required to adapt the space. If physical changes are to be made, the best way to ensure flexibility is with a structural system that minimizes the need for interior partitions. Such structures allow for easy addition or deletion of walls. Building with accessibility in mind is an important way to extend the useful life of a home should occupants become disabled. While it may not be sensible to install all elements required for accessibility, simple measures such as building-in three-foot-wide doorways and minimizing level changes will allow for an easier transition of the home should the need arise.

## Timelessness and Durability

What will become of our home in fifty, one hundred, or five hundred years? This is a question of durability, adaptability, and style, and one we don't often bother ourselves with. But, when you build to last, as green design calls for, you carry a responsibility to what the long-term impacts of your home will be. Most homes today are built to last thirty to fifty years. This is hardly a legacy worth leaving our children.

Long-term maintenance and/or replacement of homes create a tremendous burden on natural resources. There is also the question of what happens to the waste we are disposing? Many landfills are already taxed to capacity and few communities are asking for one to be placed in their backyard. Buildings of earth, such as pise or rammed earth, are built to last hundreds—if not thousands—of years, and the walls are essentially maintenance free. Material choice is not the only way to accomplish durability however. Design features such as wide overhangs, tall foundations, pest control, proper roof and site drainage, and wind breaks all contribute to the life of a building.

In addition to the notion of homes wearing out, much waste occurs due to changes in style. If we don't like the look of something anymore, we throw it out and buy a new one. While it is possible to salvage certain components for reuse, such as cabinetry or fixtures, most elements in our homes have been screwed, glued, and painted, and are difficult to disassemble for reuse

W HAT WILL IT TAKE FOR US TO ONCE AGAIN BECOME INDIGENOUS?" —WILLIAM MCDONOUGH or recycling. By designing in a timeless manner, you will reduce the amount of remodeling that would occur as a matter of taste. Timelessness does not mean that something has no perceivable style. It simply means that the home displays a level of integrity, which can mark its time in history without becoming an eyesore generations later. This can be accomplished through site-specific design. If the home responds beautifully and sensibly to its surroundings, topography, vegetation, and climate, it will remain in context for the long-term. A display of structural systems also builds in an aesthetic that will not fade in style.

# TARRYTOWN HOUSE:
# An Exercise in Efficiency

Austin, Texas, is home to an aggressive green-building program. Architect Peter Pfeiffer has developed a keen sense for what "green" design means in the twenty-first century. In his view, modern design strategies should infuse climatically appropriate comfort strategies with the latest available technologies in materials and systems. In this way, mainstream solutions can bring green design to virtually any project.

When the time came to design his own green home, Peter was well prepared for the task. At a basic level, there were the spatial requirements of a rambunctious family of six to be met. He ran his family project similar to any other client relationship, with regularly scheduled meetings to pour over sketches, models, and wish lists.

"We wanted to build a house to demonstrate that real green could still be very attractive, and that a large family could live comfortably in a good-sized (not oversized) home that would consume less energy than a typical Austin starter home," Peter says.

His intention was to not only meet his family's functional and aesthetic requirements but to create a laboratory that demonstrated his own notion of sustainable design. The result is, as Peter describes, "an award-winning country interpretation of the Craftsman architectural style infused with high technology construction techniques and serious green building strategies."

## Site

Central Texas's hot and humid climate calls for design solutions that control heat gain through windows and the building envelope and that provide ventilation to eliminate unwanted heat and moisture. The site—a mid-sized cen-

**Location:** Tarrytown, Texas
**Architect:** Barley + Pfeiffer Architects
**Owners:** Karen and Peter Pfeiffer
**Square Footage:** 4,175
**Cost:** $175 per sq. ft.
**Builder:** Oliver Custom Homes
**Photographer:** Peter Pfeiffer, AIA

FACING
*This home serves as a laboratory to demonstrate that high-tech and high-design are compatible with the goals of sustainability.*

RIGHT
*The lack of wall-to-wall carpeting and the use of low-VOC paints and finishes contribute to indoor environmental quality without sacrificing style.*

## SUSTAINABLE FEATURES

- Urban infill site
- Construction waste management
- Gray water reuse
- Native landscaping
- Passive heating and cooling design
- Appropriate size
- Tight and energy efficient building envelope
- Energy efficient mechanical systems
- Nontoxic pest control
- Use of low maintenance materials
- Use of recycled and local materials
- Healthy interior finishes

*Locally harvested limestone is a trademark of Austin, Texas, homes. It connects this home to its locale. This stone, along with fiber-reinforced cement siding, provides a durable, low maintenance exterior.*

tral city lot—was selected for its close proximity to services such as schools, church, stores, parks, and transit stops. The home is sited to take advantage of the prevailing cooling breezes and good solar orientation in such a way as to maximize passive cooling in the summer and passive solar heat gain in the winter. With its long axis running east-west, the majority of the windows face north and south. This orientation is also great for receiving the prevailing southeast breezes so the house and screened porch remain cool even on the hottest of August days.

Aspects of the site were protected or enhanced during the construction phase.

Portions of existing topsoil were harvested and stored on site for use during final grading. Debris from the site was chipped and used as mulch for soil amendment.

**Water**

Water-conservation techniques were utilized on-site with the extensive use of Xeriscape design (low water-use vegetation). Drip irrigation efficiently uses water where it is most needed. Supplemental water needs for the landscape are met by using laundry washing machine water (gray water). This is accomplished by diverting the water to a separate tank in the front yard until it is needed. A rainwater collection system provides additional landscape watering as well as operation of the cooling tower. A simple "roof washer" system diverts the initial flow of dirty water before collecting runoff in the cistern.

### Space

The layout of the interior spaces accomplishes comfort goals of heating and cooling while also being unique to the way a contemporary family lives. An open central stair tower helps cool the home while flooding its center with daylight, creating a fun backdrop for the family piano. An ample-sized casual living/dining/kitchen area, opening onto a screened porch, allows for supervised kid play and four-season enjoyment. The master suite represents a sanctuary in the trees and includes a European-style bathroom/dressing room.

### Ventilation

Windows and oversized roof overhangs throughout the home are designed and sized to provide summer shading, yet allow for ample natural lighting and natural winter heating from the sun. The windows were sized based on sun-angle calculations, which determined a balanced solution throughout the year.

Airflow is of utmost importance if one is to remain comfortable in this warm and humid climate. The operable windows are placed and arranged to provide for enhanced natural ventilation. This means that cross-ventilation is coupled with high windows that help exhaust out hot air by way of "thermal siphons." As hot air exits the home through these windows, cooler air is drawn in through ground-floor windows, positioned to take advantage of the prevailing breezes.

Warm air is recirculated within the home for comfort during the cold season. A thermostatically controlled, variable speed recirculation duct system pulls warm air from the upper level down to the lower levels, where it is needed.

### Building Envelope

Wall cavities are filled with a spray of air-sealing foam, and then filled with cellulose. Attic ceilings are also sealed with foam to create a vented roof and a sealed attic. This creates a tight building envelope, which allows for humidity control. Controlling humidity can also eliminate mold within the structure.

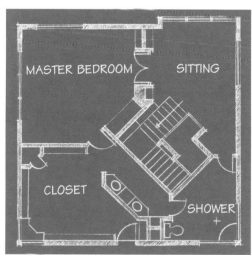

Because the bulk of energy costs in central Texas are spent on cooling the home, control of heat gain is an important strategy for reducing energy demands. The metal roof contains a self-venting radiant barrier system that consists of dual venting paths, keeping the ventilated attic temperatures close to that of the outside—40 to 50 degrees cooler than a typical attic in the area. Also, insulation board installed under the ceiling keeps the upstairs more comfortable in the summer months by providing a thermal break between the finished ceiling and the roof structure.

Extra precautions were taken during design and construction to keep the effects of sun and rain from deteriorating the home and causing future maintenance problems. The exterior wall sheathing is wrapped in a heavy-duty building wrap installed to keep moisture out of the walls. This protects the house framing from mold and wood decay while reducing the work the air conditioner has to do to humidify the home in the summer, providing a healthier indoor living environment. High quality wood-framed windows with double-pane low-E glass add to the building envelope's efficiency.

"We wanted a home that would be around for our kid's kids to inherit and enjoy," the owners say.

### Materials

The home is constructed of engineered floor trusses and microllam structural beams made from previously wasted strands of timber, along with finger-jointed 2 x 4-inch wood studs. These products use wood resources more efficiently, reducing the number of trees required to build the house.

Homes in the area are prone to termite infestation. Installing termite protection during construction eliminates the need for toxic treatments in the future. This is accomplished with Termi-Mesh nontoxic termite treatment coupled with an application of nontoxic Timbor insecticide in the wall cavities prior to the drywall installation.

Reclaimed and recycled materials were also utilized to minimize resource use and add durability to the home. Moisture-Shield synthetic exterior wood trim, from 95 percent post-consumer recycled plastic and wood chips, provides a low maintenance exterior while using resources effectively. The exterior stone Is locally quarried, reducing the "embodied energy" content of this home with the added benefit of giving the house a local texture and context.

### Energy

Peter is a firm believer in the need for optimum energy performance when building sustainable homes. A home may contain the most benign products but if it does not perform well, it will have a greater negative environmental impact for years to come. Meticulous attention to detail, from the building envelope to the mechanical system installations, enabled the construction of a high performance home. Based on extensive computer-based modeling, anticipated utility bills are roughly equivalent to homes one-third the size at approximately $200 per month total average operating costs for a five bedroom, 4000+ square foot home.

The air conditioning system's waste heat is captured for reuse. By linking the high efficiency water-cooled AC system to the swimming pool, free pool heating is provided during the fall and spring.

Instead of the conventional condensing units usually found on most residential air conditioning systems, a small cooling tower, a miniature version of the system commonly found on commercial projects, is utilized. This cooling tower employs evaporative cooling to improve efficiency; it is also locally developed and reliable. This system allows for one less gas-fired appliance in the home, further enhancing the indoor air quality. Another unique feature of the air handling system is that it provides a slight positive pressure to this home's interior, further reducing the chance for the infiltration of overly humid outside air in the summer and cold drafts in the winter.

The carefully planned and installed duct system is constructed of sealed sheet metal, maximizing even airflow throughout the house to diminish the chance of some rooms being warmer or cooler than others. This attention to detail also reduces the chance for dirt or molds to accumulate inside the ducts, and reduces duct leakage (a major source of energy waste in most homes). This results in lower energy bills and a healthier indoor air quality. Minimal use of "flex" ducting also makes for a more permanent and better sealed air-conditioning duct system.

Three separate air-conditioning systems

allow for independent zoning of the major areas of each floor, and are controlled by digital programmable thermostats. This makes for greater control of comfort, less energy consumption, and greater flexibility as living needs change over time.

Energy-efficient and water-efficient appliances were used throughout. The front-loading horizontal-axis washing machine saves water and energy and eliminates a major cause of humidity within the home, enhancing comfort and indoor air quality.

### Indoor Environmental Quality

Indoor air quality considerations were met through the detailing and selection of the mechanical system as well as the materials and products installed in the home. The foam and damp blown cellulose insulation contains no HCFC or formaldehyde. Recycled antique pine wood floors and stained concrete floors provide low-maintenance, cleanable floors. Nontoxic finishes were used, including those

with low VOC paint and woodwork finishes, and undyed natural wool carpeting. There is no wall-to-wall carpeting, which minimizes the potential for moisture condensation that may cause mildew.

Clean air is provided to the home with the installation of high-intensity ultra-violet lamps and a Space Guard pleated filter medium. This is further enhanced by the control of fresh outdoor air into the system.

A central vacuum system reduces household dust by exhausting directly to the outside, where it is vented far from the home's fresh air intakes. Electrical installations were designed to reduce the occupants' exposure to EMFs.

The experience of acting as both client and architect proved to be an insightful one for the Pfeiffers. As with many of their clients, building their dream home was to be the greatest financial investment of their lives. This perspective gave Peter a better understanding of his clients' emotions and experiences when working through the process. Additionally, he

was faced with the temptation to "do it right." Architects in his position often experience the "Honey, while we're at it . . . " phenomenon. While this added about 25 percent to their budget, they are proud of the decisions that they made.

As Peter says, "We cringe at the time, effort, and funds it cost us—but are very glad we did it right. Next to having our kids, my wife and I feel this was one of the most fulfilling exercises we have undertaken together."

### Awards

Austin Green Builder Program's 5 Star Rating. ■

**LEFT**
*Gray water is captured from the home and stored in a cistern beside the garage until it is needed in the landscape. Rainwater is also collected and utilized for landscaping needs, as well as for use in the cooling tower.*

**FAR LEFT**
*Wide overhangs protect exterior materials from deterioration and provide shading for windows at each level. The overhangs were precisely sized according to local sun angles to avoid summertime overheating.*

ABOVE
*With the look of a restored farmhouse, this new home utilizes green design techniques to meet the owners' goals for efficiency, affordability, comfort, and function for an active farming family.*

# KELLER FARMHOUSE:

# Livability

The Kellers had lived in an old, deteriorating farmhouse for thirteen years on the site of their new home. This gave them plenty of time for dreaming up an ideal home. It also gave them intimate knowledge of the site, so that when the time came to make the dream a reality, they knew exactly how to capture the best the site had to offer.

The Keller family is a nuclear one—mom, dad, and four kids from ages three to twelve. Two boys share a bedroom; the others have their own. All but the youngest help on the farm. As a family of farmers who are used to working with the rhythms of nature, the home they dreamed of had to do the same. Their vision included an energy-efficient classic farmhouse with good sunlight, hardwood floors, and a masonry heater. They wanted a home small enough to be affordable to build, operate, and maintain.

## Design

Architect selection began by thumbing through the local Yellow Pages. During the interview process it was easy for them to sense early on who they would get along with. They needed an architect to not only design their dream house but also one who would address the floodplain condition at the site of the home.

"Terry was practical from the start," the Kellers said. "She said that she wouldn't begin the design process until the floodplain issue was resolved. That impressed us."

When speaking with the owner, you can sense that she's fallen in love with her house. She attributes this to the years spent dreaming of a new home and knowing exactly what she wanted, along with the architect's thorough questioning and examination of the family's goals in the design phase. "Somehow she [the

## SUSTAINABLE FEATURES

- Floodplain design
- Vernacular design response
- Efficient space utilization
- Extended outdoor living
- Passive solar
- Masonry heater
- Heat recovery ventilator
- Hard surface floors
- Detached garage
- Durable materials

**Location:** Western Washington, east of Seattle
**Architect:** Living Shelter Design
**Owner:** Keller family
**Square Footage:** 1,392 main, 941 upper, 2,333 total
**Cost:** $230,000 for home, $33,000 for garage with unfinished apartment
**Builder:** Gordon Construction
**Photographer:** Mike Zarieki

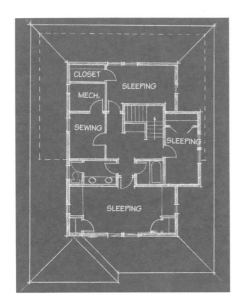

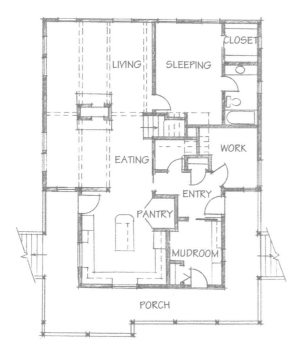

architect] was able to take our ideas, put them all together, and design a house that is just perfect for us," the owner says.

Approached from the northeast, the Keller Farmhouse appears to be a well-tended family home that has existed for generations. The wood siding and peaked roof are accented with charming shutters and a lattice base. A covered porch wraps around the east end, and partway around the north and south sides of the home. This offers year-round protection from the elements, and an invitation to relax outside or inside.

### Site

The house was sited on the footprint of the original farmhouse that was structurally past the stage of remodeling and in need of demolition. While a fixed footprint was a challenge for the architect, it was a good step toward reducing ecological impact on the site. The foundation design also reduced the impact. The floodplain was one of the major design challenges. Rather than trying to fortify the house against water damage, the architect developed an open foundation allow water to flow under the house during flooding: eight-foot-wide openings in the concrete walls on all sides allow floodwaters to pass under the house. A continuous strip footing is connected through the middle of the structure in several locations to withstand possible "liquefaction" if there happens to be a flood and an earthquake at the same time. The raised floor keeps the occupants above the wet ground when the water rises.

The site receives a substantial amount of rain throughout the year. This was a driving factor in the construction schedule which, because of the sensitivity of the floodplain condition, had to occur during the dry time of year.

### Space

As you enter the home from the north, you get a glimpse of the great room beyond, which gives the feeling of openness without sacrificing privacy. To the right is a small office, with room for two desks and built-in cabinets, and a half bath that fits neatly beneath the stairs. The mudroom has a separate entry from the east end of the porch, allowing for easy removal of muddy boots or a quick load of laundry. There is a shoe cubby and space for everyone's things, which is a unique feature in a small home, yet crucial to the farmer's way of life.

"Our friends are envious of our spacious and organized mudroom. I think it's funny how most people can't afford the luxury of a spacious mudroom like those in a more expensive home. People in those homes don't get as dirty as we do!" the owners say, laughing.

The high ceiling of the main living space is accented with exposed beams while a "Tempcast" brick fireplace creates a natural divider between the dining and living rooms, as well as a warm place to sit with guests. This creates a space that is combined yet broken up slightly to create what the owner calls a feeling of being "both cozy and open." Windows all along the south wall take in the sun and views of the surrounding mountains, while the porch overhang prevents the home from overheating in the summer. A door from the rear of the kitchen and dining area extends the living space to the porch, with stairs out to the backyard. In the corner of the living room, a small alcove creates a private intermission before the door opens into the owner's suite.

The upper living space is built into the rafter slope to avoid wasted space and materials and includes two children's bedrooms, a sleeping alcove, and one split bath. At the top of the stairway is an oversized landing that can be used as a play area. Small windows are neatly tucked beneath the eaves to bring light onto the children's beds. A small mechanical room is tucked beneath one of the four upper-floor dormers.

A matching detached garage with an upper-story mother-in-law unit completes the homestead and offers ample storage space for cars and toys, as well as an extra room for guests.

### Energy

Energy efficiency was of great importance as a means of keeping the cost of living down. Temperature control is a key factor in achieving this goal. The house was oriented east-west for passive solar gain. A masonry heater is the source of heat for the entire house. Its heat radiates from the fireplace and is very comfortable. A fire once a day is typically enough to keep the house comfortable, twice a day during the coldest part of winter.

### Materials

The structure is framed using standard 2-inch x 6-inch studs at 16-inches on center, with engineered wood trusses for floor joists and roof rafters. The rafters sit on top of the floor joists to allow for good insulation out to the perimeter. Durable materials such as Hardiplank siding (made from cement and

waste wood fiber), fiberglass windows, and ironwood decking finish the exterior. The wraparound porch provides protection from the elements and also prolongs the life of the exterior materials.

### Indoor Environmental Quality

Indoor air quality is maintained with the use of a heat recovery ventilator to efficiently exchange indoor air. The hard surface floors are easily maintained.

"We were only going to do this once in our life, so it had to be built to last. We chose quality materials throughout. The ironwood decking will likely long outlast the house," the Kellers say.

Every inch of this home is uniquely utilized to meet the needs of the growing family. At the same time, the house works with the rhythms of nature. The home was designed to

replace an old, decrepit house in dire need of repair, without losing the charm and appearance of an old farmhouse. Passersby often stop to take pictures and comment on the quaint farmhouse. Many friends even mistake the new Keller home for the farmhouse that had been there for years—except they cannot understand how it was made to look so new and beautiful. ■

BELOW

*A masonry heating fireplace defines the living spaces with a comforting ambiance while also providing the primary source of heat for the entire home.*

# SANDERS RESIDENCE:
# Healthy Living

While Christmas shopping, Martha Sanders stumbled upon Ecowise, a store featuring environmental products and information. A conversation with the proprietor and a browse through his resources opened a world of ideas of which she was previously unaware. She had been an advocate for the environment and tried to do her part by recycling and living efficiently, but she had not understood the full potential for sustainable living. Unfortunately she and her husband, Russell, had recently completed the construction of a new home. She was alarmed to learn that the materials and products she had chosen could harm her family's health. Martha was unhappy with the house from that conversation onward. As they set out to design a new home, it was clear that a whole new set of priorities would influence the design. "We just wanted a home that was healthy for our family and the environment. We didn't realize how unique this way of building was. It was a real eye-opener," Martha says.

### Site

Selecting a new home site enabled them to move closer to town where more resources would be available to their daughter. They found a two-acre lot and began taking root. Their construction process was sensitive to minimizing disturbance of the site and enhancing natural features. Re-vegetation of the septic drain field consisted of native or climatically adapted vegetation such as prairie grasses and wildflowers. Their food waste, as well as their horse's manure, feeds a compost system that fertilizes an organic garden.

### Water

Rainwater is captured from the roof in five-gallon buckets. The future installation of a catchment cistern will simplify this process; it will be added when budget allows. Water from the home is

**Location:** Buda, Texas
**Architect:** Gayle Borst, Stewardship, Inc.
**Owners:** Martha and Russell Sanders
**Square Footage:** 1,542
**Builders:** Martha and Russell Sanders
**Cost:** $112,000
**Photographer:** Gayle Borst

ABOVE
*A covered walkway between the garage and house provides protection from the elements without the threat of automobile fumes entering the living spaces.*

## SUSTAINABLE FEATURES

- Minimal construction waste
- Planting with native vegetation
- Household and farm compost to amend soil
- Rainwater use
- Salvaged materials

- Designed for efficient utilization of space and materials
- Emphasis on healthy and natural materials

used efficiently with the design of a private, outdoor shower that directs water straight into the landscaping.

### Design

The owner of Ecowise, a member of a local green-building coalition, recommended several resources including architect Gayle Borst, who was experienced in environmentally sensitive design. The owners immediately hit it off with Gayle and knew she should be the one to design their home. "Gayle didn't just design the house  she helped all the way through," the Sanders said. "When we had problems finding a material she would help with research and tracking down leads."

Initially, the owners were unsure of several design features that the architect proposed. But because they had developed a great deal of trust in her, they allowed Gayle flexibility with the design and are very pleased with the results. An example is the unique response to the owners' wish for a bay window. Such features tend to be expensive to build relative to the space gained. Gayle proposed achieving the feel of a bay window on the interior by flanking the eating area with one exterior window, and one that connects to an interior greenhouse space. The salvaged beam overhead further provides the sense of an extended space, without the added expense.

When working with limited budgets, it is important to prioritize work that is more easily done during the initial construction and those features which may be added later with ease. With this in mind, there were items that are planned for future installation when funds become available, including a rainwater cistern and a clean wood-burning stove.

*Exterior walls are built of an ICF system called Faswall, which is plastered to provide both insulation and thermal mass for a durable and efficient structure.*

FACING

*Though the home is relatively small, gestures such as clerestory windows create a feeling of a much larger space. These windows allow the owners to enjoy watching the sky change from day to night.*

## Construction

Since Martha spends her days home schooling their daughter, the family lives on one income. This meant that they needed to live and build on a budget. They attempted to achieve a goal of $65 per square foot for construction cost by building smaller, and by acting as their own general contractor. Though they did exceed their original goal, the resulting quality far exceeds the $112,000 investment.

Russell's carpentry skills and creativity with materials came in quite handy. A $5 purchase of the book *How to Be Your Own Contractor* was an investment that likely saved them thousands. Although they had built their previous home, they were unfamiliar with the green systems and materials that went into this home. Besides playing the role of general contractor, they also did much of the work themselves. By doing some of the labor-intensive finish work, they realized substantial savings.

The owners were successful in minimizing construction material waste. By sorting metals, wood, and corrugated cardboard for recycling, they never required the typical trash Dumpster. There were even sorting bins available for workers' cans and bottles, which the owners took to the recycling facility themselves. Efficient use of materials was due in large part to creative thinking. Extra wall forms were used to build a mailbox surround and footings for the horse stall, and the remaining concrete masonry units were donated to a neighbor's construction project. Faswall—a recycled wood chip and cement wall form—eliminates the need for much wood; however, there were areas such as

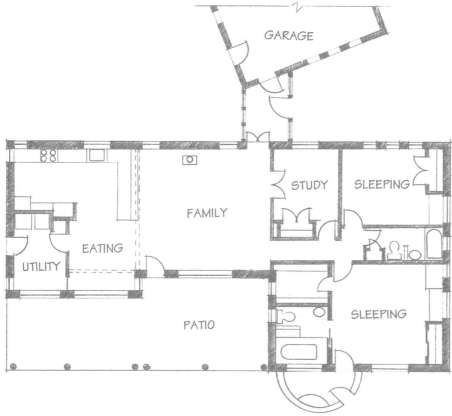

window and door openings that required temporary forming. The wood forms were recrafted into the finished window frames. Pine boards that were not needed for the ceiling finish were installed as a wainscot in the bathroom and as the finished windowsills.

### Space

An open living/dining/kitchen area was essential. Home schooling happens in the dining room near people and activity. They wanted most of the square footage of the home there, where the family could enjoy it together. This meant reducing the size of personal sleeping spaces. The patio and arbor areas expand living spaces to the south and provide protection from the summer sun.

A much enjoyed feature of the family space is the twelve-foot-high ceilings penetrated by small, high windows that show the night sky and the rising moon. The windows also provide extra daylight, and open for ventilation.

Antique weathered beams from an old cotton gin exposed at the ceiling level separate the living room and kitchen above the raised bar and define the dining "bay" window area. Martha found a hanging fixture with leaves for the bar as a way to bring nature inside through decoration.

A touch of daylight was added to the kitchen by punching small windows between the countertop and the wall cabinets. Without sacrificing storage space, the family now enjoys outside views and the sounds of birds, where there would otherwise have been a dark corner.

The living space is expandable with an adjacent room connected by salvaged French doors. This provides the flexibility of use as the study, guest bedroom, or potential third bedroom.

### Materials

Exterior walls are constructed of Faswall with unpainted lime/cement/sand stucco. This system provides both insulation and thermal mass to create an efficient, durable, and soundproof structure. Wood use is limited to temporary blocking of doors and windows.

Due to the owner's concerns with potential chemicals in compounds used in the drywalling process, not a bit of Sheetrock exists in this house. Interior walls are constructed of 4-inch concrete masonry block, which is plastered to match the exterior walls. This creates visual continuity and provides additional interior thermal mass for temperature balance. The owners applied the first coat of stucco, which was site-mixed in wheelbarrows. This proved to be a tremendous amount of work. They then decided to pay the additional cost for others to apply the finish coat. "It is meaningful to see the labor in the walls," the owners say. "Curves and indents make them unique."

Regarding their door the owners say, "The leaded-glass door to the patio was found at the Austin Habitat for Humanity's Restore for about $35. Several panes of glass were broken, so those panes were replaced and the glass panel reinforced. Then with some stripping and refinishing of the wood, we ended up with a beautiful door. At certain times of the year, the sun strikes the beveled glass circle in the middle of the door and makes rainbows in our living room."

Much of the soffit wood and many of the interior doors were salvaged, as was the clawfoot tub and the beautiful arched-top cabinet that holds the bath towels in the master bath. Martha spent many hours searching for these wonderful pieces.

### Energy

The house's design emphasized room and window placement relating to the sun, configuration for sun/shade and breezes, natural ventilation, and thermal comfort with minimal mechanical intervention. All of these features are very important on a site such as this with little shading available from existing trees.

The compact size of the home is easy to heat and cool. High-mass walls and the floor assist with summer thermal comfort by tempering the heat gained throughout the day. A high-efficiency wood stove is planned to provide most winter heating needs.

Natural light provides all lighting during the day. In the evening, energy-efficient, compact fluorescent fixtures are used as well as energy-efficient appliances. An on-demand gas water heater saves both energy and water.

The roof is insulated with R-30 cellulose, rather than the recommended R-26. The overall performance is quite a bit higher, however, with the radiant barrier and vented Galvalume roof eliminating heat gain that may otherwise penetrate interior spaces.

"During construction in the middle of the summer, Martha and Russell found that it was so comfortable working inside their house (which consisted only of concrete floors, the Faswall walls, and a roof with radiant barrier at that stage), that they asked if it was necessary to install the roof insulation. While the summertime performance of the house was impressive, I assured them they would come to appreciate the roof insulation, particularly in the winter," says the architect Gayle Borst.

### Indoor Environmental Quality

Creating a healthy living environment was a high priority for the owners. They took every measure possible to ensure that no harmful materials or finishes were installed. These priorities were met with measures such as installing concrete floors that were colored with nontoxic stain, using unfinished wood ceilings throughout, and opting against carpet, joint compound, and wood products containing formaldehyde. Additionally, a detached garage, connected to the home with a breezeway, was built to keep automobile exhaust and fumes from entering the living space.

"In my previous home, people would comment on that 'nice new home smell.' I didn't want that at all. Now all we smell is clean, fresh air," Martha says.

This home is a wonderful example of what highly motivated owners can do on a limited budget. By establishing priorities, the Sanders were able to achieve a high level of green for their home and incorporate most of their desired features. They were able to avoid almost all typical threats to healthy indoor air quality such as plastics, wood products containing formaldehyde, carpeting, joint compound and texture, and cavity walls. The resulting interior is an excellent demonstration of the healthfulness and beauty that results from the use of simple, natural materials, especially in the presence of natural light. ■

BELOW LEFT
*The owners were adamant about creating a healthful place to live and raise their family. Careful attention was paid to materials and finishes as well as to the comforting quality of the home's design.*

BELOW RIGHT
*The bathroom exhibits resourceful use of materials. The claw-foot tub was salvaged from another project. The wainscot and windowsills utilize pine boards that were not needed to finish the ceiling.*

# PADER RESIDENCE:
# Communal Living

Through years of anthropological research into the living style of Mexican cultures, Ellen Pader has developed a philosophy that dwellings represent and influence the culture of families and a larger community's political condition. For her, the design of a home helps shape the relationships inhabitants have with one another, within the family, and with society as a whole.

With a young daughter, it was important to create places for play that would remain functional as the little one grew. The single story design addresses issues of safety, supervision, and ease of movement for the five-year-old. Furthermore, it will remain a viable solution for the owner as she ages in the home.

**Location:** Northampton, MA
**Architect:** Kraus-Fitch Architects, Inc.
**Landscape Architect:** Dean Cardusis
**Owner:** Ellen Pader
**Square Footage:** 2,241
**Cost:** Not available
**Builder:** Doug Kohl, Kohl Construction, Inc.
**Photographer:** John Fabel

### Design

Architectural influences such as the work of Cliff May, a modernist architect out of Los Angeles, established firm ideas in Ellen's mind. May's work had always resonated with her, with its simple lines, sense of proportion, and functional use of space.

Ellen's landscape architect, Dean Cardasis, introduced her to architect Mary Kraus. Within minutes she knew Mary was the one for the job. She asked the right questions and seemed to easily grasp the goals Ellen had established. Ellen had come into the process well prepared with detailed lists of features she liked and disliked. According to Mary, this "made for a much more successful design process with a richer outcome."

### Site

The home is affiliated with a cohousing development, which is about a quarter-mile walk down a connecting road. The cohousing developer held aside three front lots that he agreed to sell to families on the waiting list for the cohousing project. They have access to the common house functions or they can remain autonomous if they choose.

## SUSTAINABLE FEATURES

- Cohousing community location
- Site design for outdoor living
- Preservation of mature trees
- Design for adaptability of use
- Courtyard plan with connectedness and interaction
- Passive solar design
- Energy-efficient, tight construction
- Cellulose insulation made from recycled newspaper
- Fiber-cement siding

- Healthful flooring choices: wood, stone, tile, and colored concrete
- Wood flooring from regional sources
- Daylighting strategies maximized
- Interior finishes free from VOCs
- Mechanical ventilation for health, using constant-duty bathroom fans
- High-efficiency, sealed combustion natural gas boiler for radiant floor heating

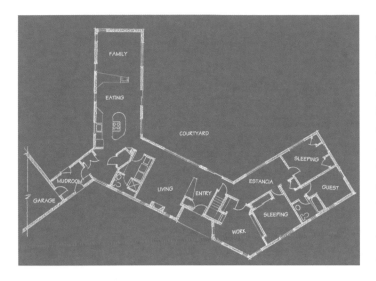

The architect and landscape architect worked closely as a team to create a setting where the house and landscape function harmoniously. Relationships between spaces are well designed to create a soft boundary between interior spaces and the outdoors. Mature existing trees remain close to the home. This conscious move was a challenge to the contractor but is an aspect that enhances the enjoyment of the outdoor living spaces and gives the home a look of belonging in its place. The resulting design is an adaptation of the traditional Mexican ranch house, with all rooms open to the courtyard, to a northeast climate.

Children's play areas were considered in the design of the landscape as well as the home. Large rocks, excavated from the home site, are a playful stage for neighborhood kids. A small gravel area bordered by these rocks is used throughout the year. In the wintertime it is filled with water to form an ice skating rink.

The patio stone is brought into the finish floor of the living area directly off of the courtyard, making it feel like the exterior corridor of the traditional ranch house. In the winter this space is filled with warm light where the children are able to continue their games of hopscotch throughout the year.

### Space

The owner's research in Mexico influenced several design concepts of this home. One is how the spaces are integrated. Each space and function is open to every other, emphasizing connection rather than separation. There are no hallways connecting point A to point B. Spaces flow into one another, but the home is not completely open. The owner intended to create connections between rooms while maintaining separate functions in clearly defined areas. The architect proposed solutions such as the divider wall between kitchen and family room, which functions as shelves on the family room side. Pocket doors dividing three distinct areas of sleeping/office, living, and kitchen/family room, when zoned off from one another, make the home function like a multistory home.

Ellen was discouraged by current trends in U.S. housing where parent's bedrooms are often isolated from children's spaces. With many homes providing private bathrooms for the children and parents, there is less opportunity for coordination and consideration of other's needs. She theorizes that this affects larger political issues, in being one important element in the creation of a culture that lacks the ability to cooperate and act responsibly toward one another.

The Estancia is a "connector" space used for many purposes such as playing or reading. The expansive windows connect this space to the outdoors as well. "The office is a wonderful shape with windows placed so that I can see someone coming and can see my daughter arriving at the bus stop," Ellen says.

At 2,300 square feet, the home is larger than originally intended; yet every space is used intensely. Her daughter's friends are comfortable in the house because there is room to run and play. Considering the lifecycle of the home, Ellen wanted to create a place that was great to grow up in as well as grow old in.

### Energy

Though the owner was not obsessive about passive solar in planning the home, the house is designed to function in relation to the sun. The south-facing courtyard exposes the home to sunlight throughout the day as the sun moves through the sky. A stone floor provides thermal mass that absorbs the sun's heat, making for a comfortable play surface during the wintertime. This comfort is enhanced by radiant in-floor heating, which the owner absolutely loves. The future installation of a trellis extending over the living room windows will contain foliage to provide shade in the summer and allow light in the winter, when the leaves drop. Abundant sunlight in the home means fewer demands for electric lighting. The building envelope is also well-insulated, using cellulose insulation made from recycled newspapers, and is tightly built to avoid infiltration heat loss.

### Indoor Environmental Quality

Paints and finishes of the home contain no VOCs, which helps protect the health of the occupants. Floors are wood, stone, and tile, which are all healthful material choices. The heating system is sealed combustion, which avoids backdrafting of combustion fumes into the interior. And the home is mechanically ventilated using constant-duty bathroom fans to ensure a consistent supply of fresh air.

The house offers many surprises. The owner finds joy in watching visitors discover the way around the house and courtyard. Though the house plan is long and linear, interesting niches and angles,

which challenged the framers, make the house "move," eliminating the stagnant nature of a linear configuration. Eight-foot-high ceilings give the spaces an appropriate proportion, which is made to feel more open through the use of natural light and bright surfaces.

This home demonstrates how one creates a dwelling that is beautiful, comfortable, and bright and that pulls people together in a world of individuality. ■

*ABOVE*

*Rather than using hallways to move from one space to another, the "Estancia" provides for open circulation. It also provides a space for other activities such as a children's play area or room for reading.*

# CHAPTER 4

# Design Specifics

It is beyond the scope of this book to detail all possible methods of utilizing your site's potential for sustainable design. However, it is essential that you have a deep understanding of your site's features and forces. To gain this understanding, you and your design team should spend a great deal of time on the site prior to putting pen to paper. Observations throughout a day, preferably even a year, will provide insight into wind and sun patterns, the changing vegetation, rainfall, existence of wildlife, ground stability, and drainage patterns. All of this information will be useful to developing the placement and design of your home.

## Site Design Recommendations

Several basic recommendations should be considered when building sustainable homes. These include making an effort to capture natural energy flows, evaluate potential hazards, connect to the community and services, design with sensitivity, and preserve and enhance natural assets.

### Capture Natural Energy Flows

● **Solar Access**
Ensure that there are no existing, or potential future, intrusions into your solar exposure. This may include adjacent structures, terrain, and mature vegetation.

● **Wind and Air Patterns**
Predominant seasonal wind patterns may be directed within a home for cooling, or diverted away for protection from the cold. Local obstructions or landforms will have an effect on these predominant flows on any given site. You should situate structures on your land in a way that takes advantage of existing vegetation for energy values, as wind or solar barriers. Use the building layout to form buffers from cold and orient to maximize solar benefits.

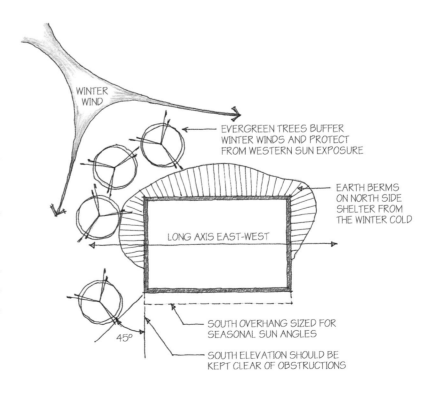

WINTER WIND

EVERGREEN TREES BUFFER WINTER WINDS AND PROTECT FROM WESTERN SUN EXPOSURE

EARTH BERMS ON NORTH SIDE SHELTER FROM THE WINTER COLD

LONG AXIS EAST-WEST

SOUTH OVERHANG SIZED FOR SEASONAL SUN ANGLES

45°

SOUTH ELEVATION SHOULD BE KEPT CLEAR OF OBSTRUCTIONS

● **Flowing Water, Rain, and Snowfall**

On-site water resources can be utilized for energy production in a micro-hydro situation, for watering landscapes, or for internal uses such as bathing or toilet flushing.

● **Earth's Energy**

The earth remains a constant temperature relative to depth below grade, within a few degrees of the climate's average annual temperature. This translates into ground temperatures that are warmer than the air in winter and cooler than the air in summer. Earth-sheltered buildings bury some of the outside walls with earth rather than leaving it exposed to air, to efficiently provide comfortable indoor temperatures throughout the year.

## Evaluate Potential Hazards

● **History**

What were the previous uses of the site? Is it pristine or was it a local dumping ground? Patterns of previous development reveal important considerations, such as the avoidance of drainage patterns, unstable soil, or undesirable wind exposures.

● **Human-made Hazards**

Look for evidence of polluted water, soil, or air. High transmission power lines or sub-stations will generate electrical fields that should be avoided.

● **Natural Hazards**

Is the site vulnerable to earthquakes or other natural disasters? Is it located in an area prone to radon, or other naturally occurring gases? If so, this is not necessarily a red flag not to build on the site, but rather information that will help you build safely and intelligently.

## Connect to Community and Services

● What is the proximity to work, school, stores, recreation, hospitals, and other commonly used resources?

● Is there access to public transit, walking, or biking to reach services?

## Design with Sensitivity

● Choose a site with a slope that accommodates the home you want rather than leveling or cutting into a slope to accommodate the house. A sloping site may lend itself to terraced, earth bermed, or walkout configurations.

## Preserve and Enhance Natural Assets

● Build on previously disturbed sites or where the least natural damage will occur. This will keep pristine areas intact while also providing an opportunity to reestablish natural vegetation, wildlife, and water flows.

● Install water efficient and low maintenance landscaping by planting with native, or climatically adapted vegetation. Arrange vegetation in groupings relative to water and maintenance needs.

● Plant edible vegetation for human and wildlife consumption.

**Efficiency**    With your decision to build green comes the inevitability of building to last. We're no longer talking about a thirty or fifty-year life span, but possibly in the range of hundreds of years. What a great legacy to leave your children and future generations. But with this legacy comes a greater responsibility for the energy used to operate your building.

Again, defining your goals for comfort in the home will help reveal an optimal solution. Some questions to ask yourself may include: Do you really crave 72-degree temperatures in each room all day long? Are there some spaces/activities that can handle more flexible temperature swings? Where should rooms be placed in order to maximize light and heat available with passive solar strategies? With such questions, you can begin to see that you have much more say over energy use than simply selecting light fixtures and appliances.

Before delving into mechanical control methods available to create comfort we must first revisit the design process. The typical approach is for the architect to complete the design, then pass it off to an engineer or mechanical installer so he or she can figure out how to heat and cool the designed building. This approach completely ignores opportunities for the architect and owner to influence energy use in the building. There are basically three steps to consider when designing for energy efficiency: (1) minimize energy needs, (2) maximize passive strategies, and (3) select the most efficient and compatible mechanical systems to achieve comfort.

## Minimize Energy Needs

A building "envelope" consists of the entire enclosure of the structure: roof, walls, windows, doors, floor, and foundation. These elements function as a building's "third skin," regulating temperature inputs and outputs. In most locations a well-insulated envelope is necessary to keep heat or cold in or out. Effects of solar gain and wind can be beneficial if the design manages them properly. These strategies are often compatible. For instance, a southern orientation will provide ample warmth during the winter months and direct summer breezes into the home while earth-coupling and trees to the north will protect the home from cold north winds. Heat gain is easily minimized by the simple cost-neutral decision to orient the building east-west. By placing the longest elevation facing south, and limiting the number of east and west facing windows, a good deal of heat gain will be avoided. While these basic strategies remain constant, the specifics of materials and configurations are dependent on each particular situation. For instance, a hot and dry climate would benefit from evaporative cooling, where comfort in a hot and humid climate is more effectively accomplished through ventilation.

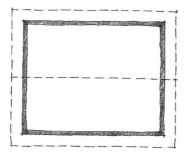

COLD CLIMATE RESPONSE:
MINIMIZE PERIMETER WALLS
TO REDUCE HEAT LOSS
THROUGH WALLS AND WINDOWS

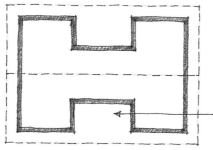

WARM-HUMID CLIMATE RESPONSE:
MAXIMIZE PERIMETER WALLS
AND WINDOWS TO INCREASE
AIR FLOW FOR COOLING

SHADED COURTYARDS HELP
TO PRE-COOL AIR USED FOR
VENTILATION.

## Maximize Passive Strategies

Buildings can assist in their own energy production by serving as a tool to collect, store, and distribute energy inputs. Best of all, this can be accomplished with the free on-site energy resources of wind and sun. While there are general patterns of wind and sun in each region, micro-climatic conditions can pose unique situations. For instance, you may live in a region that is hot and dry, but your particular site may be wooded near a stream. That would call for a design response not typical for your region.

Passive solar strategies are beneficial in any climate. You will either be inviting sun in or blocking it out. The following outline lists basic elements of passive solar design.

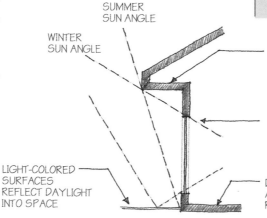

SUMMER
SUN ANGLE

WINTER
SUN ANGLE

SOUTH-FACING OVERHANGS
SIZED ACCORDING TO
SEASONAL SUN ANGLES

WINDOW HEIGHTS AND AREAS
SIZED TO MAXIMIZE PASSIVE
SOLAR OPPORTUNITIES

LIGHT-COLORED
SURFACES
REFLECT DAYLIGHT
INTO SPACE

DARK SURFACES
ABSORB SOLAR
RADIATION

## Ways to Collect Solar Energy

● **Building Orientation**

The building should run east-west to maximize the availability of south-facing glass and walls.

● **Shading**

Roof overhangs and other shading devices should be sized according to sun angles.

● **Direct Heat Gain**

This is achieved by allowing the sun to enter windows, directly warming rooms.

● **Indirect Heat Gain**

This is achieved by allowing the sun to warm a surface that will later radiate heat into the interior space, such as a Trombe wall.

● **Window Selection**

Glazing types determine the amount of heat gain available from the sun. For instance, there are some glazings that are reflective or tinted, which are appropriate on east and west faces where control with shading is difficult to attain. All windows have a designation referring to their solar heat gain coefficient (SHGC) and visible transmittance (VT) to allow for flexibility in performance based on exposures.

## Ways to Store Solar Energy

● **Insulation**

Heat gain is kept within the space through a well-insulated envelope. Windows, like building insulation, are rated with R-values for their insulating capability. In addition to the glazing, frame components contribute to the thermal performance of windows. Condensation that occurs on the inside of aluminum windows in the wintertime is due to the conductive nature of the material, making aluminum a poor choice for window frames.

● **Thermal Mass**

Floors, walls, counters, and furnishings provide opportunities for thermal mass. Whether directly or indirectly exposed to the sun's warming rays, this mass will store heat and function as a "sponge" for later distribution. This mass also tempers the effects of the sun's heat by releasing it slowly as needed.

## Ways to Distribute Solar Energy

● **Convection**

Warm air rising is a simple method of heat transfer, but only if you desire all of your heat in the upper reaches of your home. Since this is typically not the case, airflow can be directed with simple measures such as ceiling fans, or by mechanically ducting air for recirculation to lower spaces.

● **Radiation**

Radiant heat moves through material from hot to cold, and is not dependent on gravity. A material's thermal mass determines its ability or resistance to the transfer of heat. Materials such as concrete or masonry have the ability to retain heat that can be re-radiated into a space to provide comfort. The time of such a heat transfer is dependent on the material's thickness and heat capacity. In general, with the exception of water (which has the highest heat capacity), heavier materials have a higher heat capacity.

## Select Efficient Mechanical Systems

After passive strategies are maximized, it may be necessary to provide additional comfort through mechanical means. Important factors to consider include the ability to provide maximum comfort, ease of use and maintenance, efficiency of the system, and the source of energy to operate the system. Be conscious, however, not to jump to conclusions about a mechanical system even if it does meet these criteria. Experience has shown that too often, equipment is sized for worst-case scenarios, which results in oversized, inefficient systems. In a well-insulated, passive solar house, backup heating can be severely downsized and simplified.

The most comfortable heating and cooling systems are those that replicate natural systems. Radiant floors are becoming a popular heating alternative to forced air systems. Though installation costs are typically higher, these systems are chosen for their comfort, ease of use, low maintenance, and efficiency. Since radiation heats objects and mass in a room (similar to the sun's rays), radiant heat is a compatible system to use with passive solar design.

Mechanical systems may be designed to be compatible with the construction materials and systems. For instance, if you know you are installing a slab on grade to be exposed as the finished floor, it makes sense to utilize a radiant floor heating system where the slab can act as an efficient heat transfer mechanism. On the other hand, if you know you prefer wall-to-wall carpet, then perhaps radiant floors are not the best solution since much efficiency is lost due to the insulative nature of the carpet.

A certain amount of light and ventilation is required by code. This light is not only good for our physiology and psychology, but it can also save a substantial amount of energy as well. Although daylight can very easily meet all daytime lighting needs, lighting can account for a substantial portion of our electrical usage. In most cases, this can be drastically diminished with little cost and effort. First, observing the light quality in a room before turning on a switch may reveal the need for no additional light, or minimal task lighting. Though this sounds simple, too often we find ourselves in the habit of flipping on a switch whether needed or not. Secondly, the light that we do use can be provided in a number of ways. Incandescent light bulbs, which have dominated residential design, are inefficient and generate a good deal of heat. Compact fluorescent bulbs now

OPERABLE CLERESTORY WINDOWS PROVIDE LIGHT AND VENTILATION

REFLECTIVE LIGHT SHELF DIRECTS DAYLIGHT DEEP INTO THE HOME

ARTIFICIAL UPLIGHT CAN BE INTEGRATED WITH THE DAYLIGHTING SCHEME TO BRIGHTEN THE CEILING IN THE EVENING

LIGHT SHELVES ALSO PROVIDE SHADING FOR SOUTH-FACING WINDOWS DURING WARM MONTHS

come in many shapes and sizes, and are often easily installed in standard fixtures.

The Energy Guide ratings of appliances are an easy way to compare the efficiency of various models by reading the expected energy costs for each. An additional resource for selection is the Energy Star rating (provided by the EPA Energy Star program) which is free and accessible to anyone. (See resources section.) Be sure, however, when comparing energy costs, that considerations for functionality and durability are also factored into the equation. It makes little sense to purchase an efficient machine if it requires frequent maintenance or replacement.

## Smart House

A popular concept circulating through many public home tours is the concept of the "smart house." This promotes the idea that inhabitants of these homes should not be bothered with decisions such as turning on a light switch. The home knows when you will arrive, what temperature you will want, and what lighting will best respond to your mood. Our entire life may be automated if we wish—what a joy! At the same time, it rejects the notion that a home's design, natural forces, and the occupants may be in harmony. While there are instances where automated controls are appropriate, such as for thermostat settings or motion sensor and security lights, there is a point when it goes too far. This constant effort to control our environment requires a good deal of energy. What is so smart about a house that is dependent on diminishing resources?

The green smart house is one that can function and interact with its occupants to provide comfort, and that holds up to the forces of nature. An example of this is an elementary school designed by William McDonough that relies on operable windows for ventilation, which are unfortunately a rare occurrence in educational facilities today. When asked how the children would know when to open the windows, he responded by saying, "If they're getting warm, they will open the windows." Our climate has been so moderated that we sometimes forget to recognize the subtleties of our comfort levels. Green design enlivens the senses and calls upon occupants to engage in the process of controlling their comfort.

## Material

Material selection has received much attention by green designers, which has in turn pushed material suppliers to respond by providing environmentally friendly products. Material choices have far-reaching impacts, such as effects on local and distant ecosystems, pollution generated in manufacture and transportation, efficiency and durability of the structure, the health of the occupants, and aesthetics. There are literally volumes of resources listing products ranging from concrete forms to light bulbs. Selection criteria are threefold: (1) consider both positive and negative impacts to surrounding and distant natural resources, (2) provide a healthy and energizing interior for the occupants, and (3) meet the aesthetic desires of the owners. The difficulty with proper material selection is the fact that there are rarely clear-cut answers. You will likely encounter trade-offs between these issues on occasion. For instance, you may find a source for sustainably harvested wood. However transportation of this material may cause more environmental harm than use of the material would prevent (because of the consumption of fuel and the pollution generated). In many cases the use of nonrenewable synthetic products are chosen because of durability and energy efficiency, with consideration of the trade-off of long-term performance versus short-term impact.

---

## Material Selection Tips

● Use resource efficient materials such as rapidly renewable, salvaged, or recycled material.

● Use local materials to reduce transportation impacts and to stimulate local economies.

● Select healthy/nontoxic materials.

● Choose durable materials that require less frequent maintenance and replacement.

● Use materials that relate to your local climate and available resources.

● Use materials efficiently through proper design and construction methods.

● Reduce waste by modular design and handle remaining materials by salvaging or recycling.

## Construction Waste Management

Under the best circumstances the concept of construction waste would be eliminated. Creating something new should not mean the generation of a lot of garbage at the same time. Typical construction projects generate truckloads of material that is thrown away before it is ever used. Furthermore, homeowners are charged dumping fees to throw away this material in addition to the cost they have just paid to purchase it new.

Fortunately much can be done to minimize construction waste. The first step is through the design and detailing of modular systems. By sizing wall heights and lengths to allow full pieces of lumber and sheathing, for instance, leftover scraps should be greatly reduced. Incidental scraps that are generated can be mulched for use on site as soil amendment or kept for fuel to heat the home.

Salvaging materials for reuse diverts material to other projects where it may have a useful life and offset the demands for new material acquisition. Remaining items should be recycled. Most jurisdictions have facilities for wood, metal, and cardboard recycling at the very least. Others are able to recycle concrete, asphalt, carpet, drywall, and paint.

## Wall Types

In addition to general considerations of material selection, it is important to give special attention to wall type selection. It is a decision that should be made relatively early on in the design process. Proper choices will help to create an integrated design that maximizes passive resources and informes the aesthetic and form of the structure.

Even the experts of Disneyland can't concoct a proper substitute for the real thing. If you want the look of an earth house, you will have to build with earth. If you want the look of a wood house, you will have to build with wood. When you travel through the older neighborhoods of any town you will notice a certain texture and style of the homes. While they may demonstrate much variety in the way of style, you can see a common bond through their response to local materials and climatic influences, which creates a regional style.

Standard small-scale construction projects usually call for wood frame with layers of materials including interior drywall, vapor barrier, insulation, exterior sheathing, exterior moisture barrier, external finish material, and trim work. These materials are commonplace for most contractors and sub trades who prefer to build in this manner due to familiarity and skill with such systems. I suggest, however, that you consider more than just aesthetics and convenience when selecting wall types or making any other decisions about materials.

Photo © Sue Barnett, Architect

ABOVE

*Rammed earth construction, while labor-intensive to install, provides a natural, durable, and beautiful structure that will stand the test of time.*

## What Materials Can Do for You

Clients often concern themselves only with the materials they will see in the final product and are less concerned with the nuts and bolts, so to speak. Yet, if you've ever experienced squeaky floors, drafty windows, or noisy pipes, you realize that these nuts and bolts have an impact on the enjoyment of your home. By designing a sustainable home you'll also have the assurance that you are doing less harm to the planet and your family. That should make us all sleep a bit easier.

## Wood Frame

Wood is a natural material with several characteristics that make it a preferable construction material. It may be a renewable resource (if managed properly), is easily worked with, and has favorable structural qualities. In addition, if treated properly, it does not pose severe health problems.

Several issues, however, do create problems that should be taken into consideration. The first has to do with our reengineering wood to enhance its natural properties by adding toxic and unhealthy chemicals. We treat sill plates with toxic arsenic treatments to reduce rot, we glue and laminate it with formaldehyde resins in order to improve strength, and we use a chipped and glued method to reduce strain on a diminishing resource. Alternative processes are readily available on the market, but it takes thoroughness to ensure that one of the more harmful products doesn't slip between the cracks.

Other problems with wood are its flammability, shrinkage, warping, and insect and rodent infestations. Also, as mentioned above, wood requires a significant amount of additional material to create a complete wall system, and each has a set of issues to be addressed. Unless special detailing is provided, thermal bridging will occur at each stud location, causing the overall insulation capacity of the wall system to be diminished. One way that green builders utilize wood more effectively is the use of advanced framing techniques. This is a method of installing 2 x 6 framing at 24-inch on center rather than 16-inch on center with a single top plate. This simultaneously cuts down on the amount of wood required and the number of thermal bridges.

## Steel Frame

Steel framing material is typically a light gauge metal composed of at least 25 percent recycled product. Unlike wood, members are manufactured to uniform sections, making it easy to achieve a plumb and square building. Similar to wood framing, steel framing also has the problem of thermal bridging, and finished walls require layers of additional material.

The cost of steel framing is typically higher than wood framing but the benefits are its durability and resistance to rot and pests. Indoor environmental quality may be negatively affected, however. If wiring is not installed properly, electric currents may flow through the structure, thereby causing occupants to run the risk of long-term exposure to hidden electrical fields.

## Natural Alternatives

Natural ways of building today are categorized as "alternative" although most have a proven history spanning generations. As a culture we have simply forgotten our native ways and have become more reliant on the "experts" of the trade. The reasons for this perception are complex. It is in part due to the general public's lack of understanding and experience in the current construction field. In addition, the building industry has influenced building codes in an effort to standardize mass production. In this way, emphasis has been placed on product performance, and human impact has become secondary. In reality these recent building methods are quite experimental since the long-term effects of such systems are only recently revealing themselves with illnesses, lawsuits, and product failures. The following methods have been tried and tested and have stood the test of time.

## Rammed Earth

Rammed earth construction consists of conveying a moist mixture of soil, water, and cement into 2-foot forms then pneumatically compacting the mixture in lifts to create a monolithic wall structure. This may involve using local site soils if they are suitable, which can greatly reduce demands on distant resources. The thick walls are durable and low maintenance, provide an aesthetically pleasing finish, and provide thermal mass necessary for proper passive solar design integration.

This system is most appropriate in mild climates with little demand for insulation and high summertime diurnal temperatures, which allows the mass to store heat from the day and then cool on summer evenings. Visual interest can be added by stratifying layers of colors in the ramming process, creating a beautiful layered look similar to a natural sand-bed formation.

Rammed earth is an equipment intensive process with specialized skill required. However, there are traveling construction crews from the southwest that are capable of installing these systems or training local crews in the method. A factor of scale may be an issue here because the larger the project, the more cost-effective it will be to have the walls formed and poured.

## PISE

Pneumatically Impacted Stabilized Earth (PISE) is a spin-off of rammed earth in an attempt to decrease construction time and cost, and allow for installation of insulation and reinforcement if needed. PISE is constructed via a single form onto which the earthen mixture is spray-applied (similar to the gunite process) then troweled to create a smooth finish surface on each exposed side.

This method has been used in cool climates due to the needed addition of insulation, and in seismic zones where the addition of reinforcement is necessary. PISE is suitable for most climates. While the exposed finish will be earth on interior and exterior surfaces, creating a monolithic look, you cannot achieve the stratified layers that are possible with rammed earth and cast earth. Special equipment and skill is also required.

## Cast Earth

Cast earth is a relatively new method. With similarities to both rammed earth and PISE methods, it requires a double form 2-foot wide into which a wet slurry of earth and gypsum (vs. portland cement) is poured (rather than rammed). This allows for insulation and reinforcement to be placed in the wall.

As with PISE, this system can be used in most climates and will allow for stratified layers of colored earth for a finished wall. Cast earth is currently struggling with proprietary constraints, which should be overcome in the near future.

Photo © Angela Dean

ABOVE

*Many green building methods are conducive to owner-built projects. Here, a team of twelve places the walls of a 1,200-square-foot straw bale structure in a weekend.*

## Straw Bale

Straw bale (not to be confused with hay bale) had its beginnings in the U.S. in the late 1800s. It emerged in the plains of Nebraska due to lack of available timber in the region. These load-bearing structures have withstood the test of time showing little or no damage despite the lack of technical engineering expertise.

The straw bales are stacked in a running bond fashion, then plastered on the interior and exterior with a natural mixture of clay, sand, water, and straw. Cement-based plasters have been used but are not recommended due to their inflexible nature and tendency to retain moisture.

Key construction issues with straw, as with most natural building materials (including wood) are the avoidance of moisture in the walls. There are several known procedures on how to detail and construct the walls to protect from moisture. Consideration must also be given to the pre-built nature of the bales, i.e., protecting them during transportation and storage.

There are essentially two major methods of straw bale construction, with slight variations and combinations possible. Load bearing, as was done in Nebraska in the late 1800s, relies on the straw itself to carry the roof loads. While this is the most efficient use of material—eliminating the need for wood—this system is not often used today. Design constraints lie in the fact that there are limits to the number and width of window and door openings. Since most of the modern structures being built also incorporate passive solar strategies, requiring expanses of glass, load-bearing straw bale construction is less than ideal.

The second, more common method is post-and-beam structure with straw as an infill material. In this case, the straw is not relied upon for structural purposes and a greater variation of walls to openings, as well as building configurations, are possible. Acquiring permits is usually quite easy with an engineered post-and-beam system. The straw becomes the thermal skin providing insulation values in the range of R-25 to R-50 (depending on who you ask). Two or three string bales may be used depending on the insulation levels and wall thickness desired.

Finished with natural plasters, straw bale walls create a comforting, soft enclosure of space that is more organic in nature than formed systems. Some people with straw bale homes have decided not to hang artwork on their walls because "the walls themselves are a work of art."

If constructed properly, the structure should require little maintenance. If a crack in the plaster does occur it can be patched with the same natural composition of the original finish.

Ease of construction may be one of the most appealing qualities of post-and-beam straw bale. Unlike the previous earth methods, no special machinery or skill is required. It is a process often employed by groups as a "barn raising" event, bringing together people of different ages, and abilities. There should be a "director" for the wall raising with close attention to detailing to pull it off effectively. Hiring a contractor to build is always an option, however you will not realize the tremendous cost savings that can occur with this system if you do. Material cost is low but the number of hands required is high. You would be paying top dollar contractor wages for simple unskilled labor tasks.

Post-and-beam structure straw bale is viable in most climates and has been built in zones ranging from the desert southwest to Alaska to the east coast. Considerations remain the same: keep water away from the walls.

## Straw-Clay

Straw-clay is a nonstructural wall system that offers both insulation and thermal mass. Loose straw is coated with clay slurry, which provides fire resistance. The straw provides the insulation, approximately R-25 for a 12-inch wall.

Straw-clay can be installed in cavities of framed walls or in conjunction with a post-and-beam system. Forms are placed temporarily until the mixture is compacted into place. Once the forms are removed, the wall requires drying time, then may be finished with plaster or conventional siding.

## Cob

This is a handmade process involving a mixture of straw and mud that is hand molded into "loafs" that are placed to form a wall. The material is laid directly over foundation systems and is itself used as a structural wall with no need for wood posts or framing. For this reason, obtaining permits may be difficult in some jurisdictions.

This system provides both thermal mass and insulation and is best accommodated for small, organic forms. However, it has also been used to build multiple stories. As with straw bale construction, cob buildings are easily constructed with no special machinery or skill required. There are special techniques, however, that one should be aware of. Printed materials, as well as the names of individuals experienced in the technique, are an invaluable resource (see Resource section).

## Fabricated Systems

For those more technically inclined there are systems that have become mainstream that have positive environmental benefits. While they may not be as naturally based as those previously discussed, there are qualities that make them desirable, including energy efficiency, ease of construction, and durability.

## SIP

Structural Insulated Panels (SIP) are prefabricated sheets of insulation board with sheathing adhered to each side. They are available in widths of 4 feet and lengths of 8 feet to 24 feet. Commonly available panels consist of a core of expanded polystyrene (EPS) with oriented strand board (OSB) glued to each side. EPS is expanded with non-CFC or HCFC gasses and is typically used in natural building due to its high efficiency and reduced wood use. SIPs with a pressed straw core is also available as an alternative.

SIPs are widely available and may be cost-competitive to standard practices depending on the design of the home. A great deal of labor can be saved because of the fact that one panel combines structure, sheathing, and insulation all in one product. This saves several steps compared to typical frame construction.

Photo © Angela Dean

ABOVE

*Straw-clay walls allow for a variety of building designs and wall configurations. Shown here are the walls prior to plaster application. The roof structure consists of wood truss joists, which use less wood than standard dimensional lumber.*

## Indoor Environmental Quality Tips

- Avoid harmful materials and finishes in your home.
- Avoid exposure to electrical installations and equipment, especially in sleeping areas.
- Control noise from the outside as well as between rooms and floors.
- Provide for optimum thermal comfort.
- Provide for daylight and views.
- Enhance sensory experience through color and texture.
- Properly vent equipment and appliances to the outside.

## ICF

Insulated Concrete Forms (ICF) are blocks or panels made of various insulating materials into which concrete and reinforcing is placed to add structural capabilities. These forms stay in place and are finished with any number of products. The insulation material may consist of EPS, or in some cases recycled materials such as wood chips. While concrete creates a durable wall system, there is a downside. Concrete uses portland cement, which is very energy-intensive to produce. However a quantity of this embodied energy can be offset by the use of fly ash (a waste product of coal firing) to replace a percentage of portland cement in the concrete.

The finished product creates a very durable, energy-efficient, and sound-resistant structure. In some cases the insulation material can function as a breathable wall, a natural means to achieving indoor air quality.

## Indoor Environmental Quality

If our home is to be a place of rejuvenation, relaxation, and soul enrichment then it stands to reason that this place should not harm us in any way. In an attempt to create a relaxing surrounding with finishes and items that tune us into natural rhythms, we may be inadvertently creating a toxic soup, which ultimately makes us sick. We should be aware of what goes into our bodies and minds. Products that are known to emit harmful substances include paints and finishes, floor coverings, adhesives, cabinetry, furnishings, and fabrics.

On average, 90% of our time is spent indoors and the majority of that time is in our own homes. In response to rising energy concerns, buildings are constructed tighter than ever, reducing the amount of fresh air let into our homes. Coupled with this is the fact that we are increasingly installing products that cause ill side effects, in some cases creating indoor air quality that is 20 to 30 times more toxic than outdoor air. Of approximately 80,000 chemicals used to make up our built surroundings, only 10% have been tested with regard to human and environmental systems. In addition, there has been little testing as to the combined effects these chemicals may have. It is a disturbing fact that we are indeed guinea pigs to the producers and distributors of products and merchandise. There has been an acceptance of ignorance on the part of manufacturers. They claim that because a material has not been proven to be harmful it should remain in use. A more appropriate system would be a precautionary approach, placing the burden of proof that the product is not harmful on the manufacturer. We cannot take for granted that someone else is protecting our best interest; we must become informed citizens of the market.

In comparison to the amount of food and drink we consume, we take into our bodies a much greater amount of air, inhaling up to 3,000 gallons of air per day. Yet how much time do we spend determining the contents of materials we use in relation to time spent considering the nutritional value of our consumables? Material selection should be similar to reading nutrition labels to verify healthfulness. Compare your home to a meal that someone has prepared for you.

**Option 1:**

How would you respond if someone prepared a meal for you and told you that some of the ingredients are known to be harmful, but only if you eat a lot of them, while others have not yet been proven to be harmful so they included them anyway. What if they said most of the ingredients have been processed to the point that you can no longer determine their original state. The food may look palatable but it would likely make you sick.

**Option 2:**

Someone prepared you a meal made from locally grown produce without the use of harmful pesticides or additives. It is rich in beneficial vitamins and minerals and will leave you feeling more energized.

Since we are not all material scientists, what can we do to ensure a healthy home? Included in the resource section are several organizations and materials to help. See the sidebar for design considerations for creating healthy indoor environmental quality.

## Avoidance

The first measure in dealing with concerns about indoor air quality is avoidance. If we can avoid the need for a material, then we need not be concerned with its effects.

- One example of this is with carpet installations. There are multiple considerations with carpet selection. You must be certain that the material of the carpet, backing, and pad or adhesives will not off-gas harmful chemicals. Even natural products such as wool may be laced with pesticides and fungicides. Then there are considerations of use and maintenance. Carpet is difficult to clean and tends to harbor dust and trap pollutants. Vacuums may take away visible dirt but the fine particles that cause irritation remain. In this case, avoidance of a product will resolve many issues that may take a substantial amount of time to resolve.

- Attached garages are another source of indoor pollutants that can be avoided. Garages are typically a storage facility for numerous hazardous chemicals that should be nowhere near your living area. In addition, vehicle fumes and leaks can contribute to contaminated air. Most homes locate the attached garage just off of the kitchen for convenience, however each time we open the door, we are allowing harmful fumes to enter. Avoidance in this case would be to design the home with a detached garage, with a weather protected walkway if necessary. Another measure would be the careful selection of weather stripping a tight doorway, and adequate mechanical ventilation of the garage.

## Healthy Options

It is possible to build your home with healthy materials and finishes. Some products require ordering from a specialty supplier while others may be found at your local hardware store.

The following tips will guide you in the selection process:
- Use water-based or solvent-free finishes rather than solvent based.
- Use products that contain no or low levels of volatile organic compounds (VOCs).
- Use cleaning products that are biodegradable and nonharmful to ecosystems.
- Avoid products that require hazardous waste disposal.
- Avoid products containing urea formaldehyde.
- Avoid the use of PVC.
- Avoid products that contain ozone-depleting compounds, including chlorofluorocarbons (CFCs).

● Radon is a soil gas common in many parts of the U.S. It causes minor to severe health problems at certain levels of exposure. Avoidance of this gas in the home is easy addressed during construction, but can be difficult in a retrofit situation. It is difficult to assess the level of radon that may occur in a home before it is constructed, making site testing somewhat irrelevant. The act of disturbing a site for construction may activate a path for radon that was otherwise undetected. In addition, spaces built below grade act as a siphon to direct the gas in concentrated levels within the home. For these reasons it should be standard practice to construct proper venting on every project in regions where radon may occur.

● Electro-magnetic fields (EMFs) are both naturally occurring and man-made. They have been found to pose health threats under certain conditions or with prolonged exposure. Within the home, there are numerous opportunities for EMFs to affect us, from the appliances that we operate to the wiring within the walls.

● Volatile Organic Compounds (VOCs) are off-gassed from a variety of products and can easily be avoided. The surge of green products on the market has created a challenging situation for the conscious consumer. In an effort to use resources efficiently, many manufacturers are now producing building components made of composite materials that often use binders containing unhealthy chemicals. VOCs are both naturally occurring (in wood terpines) and synthetically occurring (from petrochemicals). They are "volatile" due to the ease that vapors are released into the air. This is referred to as off-gassing of products that tend to have a noticeable "new" smell and are typically found in manufactured wood products, paints and coatings, carpeting, synthetic fabric, and sealants. Health impacts of exposure range from irritability and headaches to chronic infections, depression, and memory loss.

If you use a manufactured product, the company making the product has a responsibility to disclose its contents in the form of a Material Safety Data Sheet (MSDS). In addition to listing key components, there is also information about handling, cleanup, and disposal. Companies are not, however, required to disclose secret formulas or ingredients that are below a certain quantity. This makes it difficult to ascertain whether or not a product is entirely safe. Common sense tells you that if the product calls for extraneous protective clothing and disposal methods, it is probably not safe. Conversely, if you can use or apply the product with standard care and clean up with soap and water, you are dealing with a much safer product.

## Elimination

Unless you are extremely cautious about all of the furnishings, cleaning products, animals, and people that enter your home, you will likely encounter pollutants that should be eliminated. Proper indoor air quality requires a certain amount of fresh air. This is an area where current energy standards and indoor air quality needs sometimes collide.

Fifty percent of a home's heat loss typically occurs through air leakage, so it is easy to see how sealing these problem areas will save a great deal of energy. However, to maintain health, we require a certain amount of fresh air. Design standards have been established as a means of striking a balance between human health and energy efficiency. Recommended levels are for 0.34 ACH (air change per hour), which translates into the air in the home being replaced every three hours. In a super tight home, air change may occur at a rate of six hours or more, which is the amount of time that indoor pollutants will remain in circulation. In many existing homes air change is achieved by opening windows during temperate months, but it may also be accomplished in harsher times simply by the opening and closing of exterior doors along with air leaks through penetrations on exterior walls and poor weather stripping. There are cases when sealing air leaks in a home may do you more harm than good. The best recommendation is to have a blower-door test performed by a certified specialist in order to determine your current air exchange and to locate potential problem areas. Resources for these specialists can be found in the Resource section of this book. With new construction, there are two schools of thought when it comes to maintenance of indoor air quality. There is agreement that fresh air is required for health; it is the means that is disputed.

One school of thought claims that by tightly sealing the enclosure energy performance will increase. Mechanical means are then necessary to provide the proper air exchange. This method is supported by the standard practice of installing a vapor barrier on either the inside or outside of insulation, depending on climate, to completely enclose the space in a nonbreathable system. Careful attention is paid to sealing openings and penetrations against possible air intrusions. During temperate seasons, air exchange may happen through open windows. During heating or cooling periods the air exchange occurs mechanically by bringing in outside air while exhausting indoor air. Energy or Heat Recovery Ventilators are an efficient means to accomplish this. During the heating season, heat from exhausted indoor air is captured and used to preheat cold outside air before it enters the space, with the converse occurring during the cooling period. These systems may be compact, quiet, and easy to install.

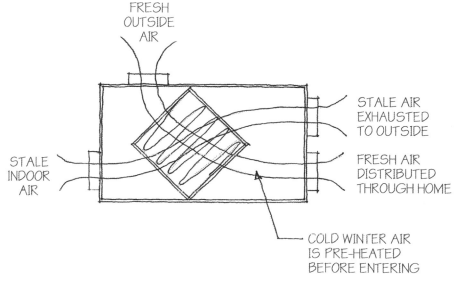

FRESH
OUTSIDE
AIR

STALE AIR
EXHAUSTED
TO OUTSIDE

FRESH AIR
DISTRIBUTED
THROUGH HOME

STALE
INDOOR
AIR

COLD WINTER AIR
IS PRE-HEATED
BEFORE ENTERING

Another method promotes achieving indoor air quality by diffusion through the building envelope via a nonsealed, "breathable" wall. This is not an effective air exchange, as would be provided mechanically, but serves to eliminate unwanted moisture and vapor. This system is best suited to more temperate climates where fresh air may be brought in through operable doors and windows during much of the year. It does not promote leaving air leaks or points where air may escape or enter directly, but also pays careful attention to weather stripping and sealing penetrations. This technique relies on proper selection of materials that are capable of slowly regulating the expulsion of pollutants while simultaneously allowing fresh air to diffuse through the wall. Some examples of wall systems that accomplish this are straw bale, strawclay, and some insulated concrete forms with natural plasters.

**Location:** Napa Valley, California
**Architect:** Paul Okamoto, Okamoto Saijo Architecture
**Owners:** George, Peter, and Ariel Rubissow, and Joyce Carlyle
**Square Footage:** 1,200
**Builder:** Geoff Austin, Leeward Construction
**Cost:** $170,000
**Photographer:** Janet Delaney

# RUBISSOW FARMHOUSE:
# Use of Materials

On a forested knoll overlooking the lush valleys and rolling vineyards of Napa Valley, an adult brother and sister, and their families, are given a little piece of paradise. The home is just a short distance from their father's home, and the "padrone" had one requirement: "Don't disturb my view from the farmhouse." The siblings had a few requirements of their own. With two separate families, privacy between personal bedroom spaces was of great importance. The shared realm necessitated an open informal living area that would be sizable enough for large gatherings yet quaint enough for one family's

use. As city dwellers with children, this place in the country was to provide the kids with balance, a place where their minds and bodies could roam.

Building as ecologically as possible within a modest budget was the driving force behind the design of this small farmhouse. Two ecological design concepts were the basis for this residence: (1) passive solar design, and (2) inventive use of recycled building materials. By focusing on these two concepts, the resulting design created open spaces that seem larger than the net floor area and finish details that seem more expensive than the

construction budget allowed.

With the limitations of a steep drop-off to the south, zoning setback limits to the north, and the need to be tucked away out of site, the architect faced a unique design challenge. Fortunately, this challenge was compatible with the goals of building a small, passive solar house with minimal visual impact.

## Space

The owners desired plenty of light and comfort in winter, which is compatible with passive solar strategies. Although the primary view is toward Mount Veeder to the west, they did not

## SUSTAINABLE FEATURES

- Minimized construction impact
- Construction waste management
- Compact site responsive design
- Passive solar design
- Integrated comfort strategies
- Use of recycled, healthy, and durable materials
- Use of earth wall system

FACING

*Minimal west windows frame an impressive view as the dominant orientation faces south for optimum passive solar control. The zigzag configuration creates privacy on the interior between sleeping zones and useful courtyards outdoors to the north and south.*

BELOW

*The view from the main farmhouse is preserved as the subtle colors and simple lines of the new home blend harmoniously with the landscape.*

want to sacrifice the comfort and natural light that a southern exposure would offer. So the building is oriented south and slightly west with a few strategically placed windows on the west elevations that offer framed views without excessive solar gain.

The home's zigzag configuration was dictated by the desire for auditory and visual privacy between those sharing the home. This creates nice pockets of exterior living space for enjoying the site while expanding the usable space. Dutch doors further the connection between indoors and out.

The children's area is located on a mezzanine loft over the great room. The south-facing shed roof provides for daylight deep within the great room and onto the mass of the earth wall. The use of this space within the roof form is essentially free, with the addition of floor structure. The kids have added innovations of their own, including a pulley and bucket system for gathering supplies needed in the loft.

The home's configuration, with its connected small spaces, allows it to blend nicely with the site, meeting the requirement for low visual impact. Upon entering the vineyard and site of the main farmhouse, this home is barely visible.

With its sleek modern style, including smooth earth walls, exposed structure, and concrete floors, the home still has a feeling of warmth provided by the texture of materials such as the salvaged wood doors, wheatboard cabinets, and the natural and playful colors used throughout.

### Energy

The local climate is not only conducive for vineyards, but is also ideal for passive solar design. Evening breezes help cool the interior during the summer while solar radiation warms the stained concrete slab floor during the winter.

The keys to this successful passive solar design include a proper balance of thermal mass, south-facing windows, sun shading roof eaves, natural cross-ventilation, and a highly insulated building envelope. Major building elevations are oriented south for optimum solar exposure, while the stained concrete slab floor and earth walls provide thermal mass. Cellulose insulation fills the building stud walls and ceilings, adding higher R-values than ordinary fiberglass batt.

An in-floor radiant heating system powered by the building's water heater and distributed in the stained concrete floor slab provides supplemental heating. This system is plumbed for the addition of solar water heating in the future.

### Materials

The availability of new and innovative recycled building materials inspired creative detailing and juxtapositions. The 18-inch thick earth walls contrast with horizontal fiber-reinforced cement siding on the exterior walls, while sheet metal flashing separates siding from wood panels. Inside, the bathroom vanity counter is made of recycled glass chips poured into a cement slab.

Wood use was minimized and used efficiently throughout the construction and finish detailing. Tall redwood doors made from an old water tank divide the private rooms from the central great room. The earth walls and fiber-cement exterior siding provide a durable and maintenance-free exterior. The interior walls, cabinets, and trim incorporate painted oriented strand board (OSB) and wheatboard. Low VOC interior paints

RIGHT

*The children's loft is easily supervised by adults below. Expansive windows provide the kids with light and views of the countryside that contrast with their weekday lives in the city.*

FAR RIGHT

*The simple form and clean lines are representative of the architect's affinity for modern design, yet the home's design remains responsive to the vernacular of the farm setting*

BELOW

*The monolithic walls of the PISE system offer both beauty and function. The sun's rays, absorbed by the massive walls, warm the space during the cooler evenings. The interior wood doors are made from a salvaged water tank; they further enhance the rich texture and colors of the interior.*

Photo by Angela Dean

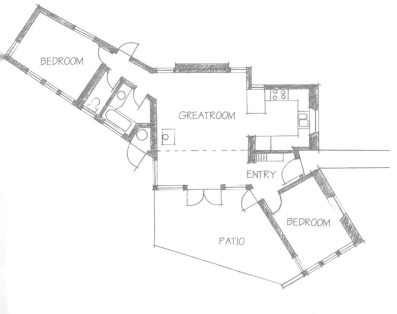

and formaldehyde-free composites provide for a healthy interior. Reclaimed redwood beams support the children's loft and solar sun shading.

PISE was used for both aesthetic and passive solar design reasons. The solid earth walls provide an integral structural finish material that does not use trees and lends a feeling of permanent, solid construction. The design idea of the PISE earth walls creates a centered feeling of home, similar to the American tradition of the hearth and masonry fireplace (Frank Lloyd Wright's Prairie Style). With the architect's modernist leanings, PISE provides an alternative to concrete as a dominant material of modern architecture, with the notion of earth as the structural material of a future sustainable design. At the same time, PISE was used in a functional way as part of the thermal mass strategy.

### Construction

The sensitive nature of vineyards necessitated careful dust mitigation during construction. This was facilitated by a design that sat on grade with minimal site disturbance.

Construction waste management practices minimized the amount of material sent to the landfill. The general contractor recycled all material packaging—cardboard, metal, plastics, and so on. He also reused the concrete plywood formwork as the plywood shear panels. The process of applying the PISE system produces excess material that does not make it into the forms. This material was quickly moved in wheelbarrows to the courtyard before hardening occurred, and formed in place to create the patio.

Though their budget was limited, the family's desires were many. Yet this did not seem to be a barrier. Through thoughtful design and innovative use of inexpensive materials, their goals were met with grace and beauty. The house was presented to Ariel on her fortieth birthday—one she will never forget. ■

## BARNETT RESIDENCE:

# Timelessness and Durability

**Location:** Central Texas Hill Country
**Architect:** Sue Barnett
**Owner:** Sue Barnett
**Square Footage:** 1,800
**Cost:** Not available
**Builder:** William Moore Construction
**Photographer:** Sue Barnett

As an architect practicing green design since the early 1990s, Sue was well prepared to design a model of sustainability. Years of designing, specifying, and recommending strategies for her clients created a desire to "walk the talk." She also wanted to push the envelope by experimenting with systems and materials so that the home would function as a laboratory of ideas to be used in future projects.

She had previously lived in an old bungalow in town, where utility bills to keep the home comfortable, and to provide ongoing maintenance, were quite high. A new, energy-efficient home would provide freedom from the financial stress of that situation. The construction also would be economical, as the time had come to call in favors from contractors and suppliers from her network over the years.

From her first experience with a rammed earth building, she knew immediately that it was the material for her. Growing up in Turkey, she was surrounded by earth buildings that had existed for centuries. Rammed earth construction resonated with her, and was a clear choice for the design of her new home.

ABOVE
*The rammed earth walls of the home are warm and energy efficient. They create an aesthetic that is only achievable with the honest use of natural materials.*

LEFT

*The open plan functions well for a single person and facilitates airflow through the home. By locating the duct work in the conditioned space, the possibility of energy losses that can occur when duct work is located in crawl spaces and attics is eliminated.*

BELOW

*An exposed ceiling structure minimizes the use of finish materials while adding the warmth of wood to the palate of natural finishes.*

## SUSTAINABLE FEATURES

- Passive solar design
- Aerobic waste treatment
- Rammed earth construction
- Minimized material use through design
- Solar hot water system
- Efficient heating and cooling strategies
- Efficient appliances and equipment

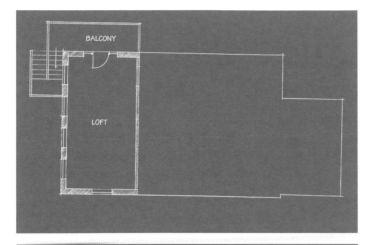

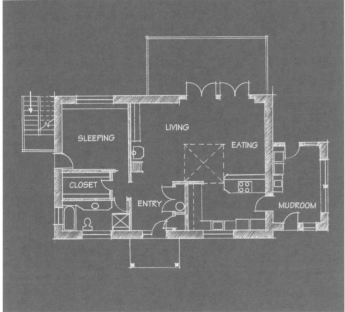

ABOVE RIGHT
*The kitchen displays material, energy, and water efficiency; appliances were selected based on energy and water-efficiency ratings. Countertops were salvaged and are inert, providing no indoor environmental problems.*

She says, "I adore the walls—they are absolutely gorgeous. I stare at them for hours on end."

## Site

The neighborhood is unique, surrounded by dedicated parkland that includes a river, natural springs, a cave, and nature preserves. The subdivision consists of one-acre sites with strict setbacks limiting building placement and orientation. This is a hot climate that receives 32 inches of rain a year; however, water availability is a concern. It is not uncommon for a single storm to deliver half of the year's total, making for relatively dry conditions the rest of the year.

On-site aerobic sewage treatment provides water for the landscape and a future rainwater capture system will further manage water shortages. The aerobic system consists of a below-ground handling tank where solid waste is digested by bacteria that is kept alive with oxygen. Water from this system flows through three chambers where it becomes successively cleaner until it is discharged onto the landscape as clean water.

### Materials

Sue set out to use as few materials as possible. The solid earth walls are monolithic, which eliminates the many layers of conventional systems. The colored concrete floor slab also eliminates the need for added flooring material. The loft structure, consisting of exposed salvaged beams and decking, serves not only as the floor but also as the ceiling below—reducing the amount of drywall used. The plan is open, with few interior walls. Trim work is limited to the tops of the rammed earth walls, which are trimmed with salvaged wood to provide a transition to the ceiling.

The earth walls, Galvalume roof, and prefinished aluminum-clad windows provide a durable shell that will be easily maintained over the years.

When incorporating salvaged materials, the end result is often quite different than if selecting new. Although the synthetic slate counter material is likely not the most environmentally friendly product with regard to production, Sue says, "I figure if it's pulled out of a Dumpster, I'm doing more good than harm. Besides, it is now an inert product, so there won't be any off-gassing implications."

### Water

The pattern of intense rainfall followed by dryness in this area makes capture and use of water quite tricky. This situation calls for an oversized cistern that will support the storage of a heavy downfall, with the ability to evenly distribute the water through many dry months. Since water is such a precious commodity in the area, this is a feature that Sue plans to add in the near future.

There was an existing well on site that is being utilized until the rainwater cistern is in place. This water is quite hard and requires treatment to minimize wear and tear on fixtures and equipment caused by mineral buildup. Sue experimented with several new technologies, but none of them worked well. She finally installed a conventional saltwater system that uses potassium rather than sodium, and hasn't had a problem since.

A solar hot water system provides the domestic hot water. This is used conservatively with the installation of a Metlund hot water circulating system. Each tap displays the availability of hot water to eliminate waste while waiting for the right temperature. This system can be retrofitted into existing structures as well as built in new.

### Energy

Sue is very pleased with the energy performance of the home. Although this house is a bit larger than her previous bungalow, the operating costs are much less. In addition to passive solar heating, an efficient wood stove with a catalytic converter provides winter comfort. Cooling strategies incorporate ventilation by inviting cool breezes from the river below. The air exits by way of the chimney effect through the home's upper story and cupola. Supplemental cooling is provided with an energy-efficient air-to-air heat pump that uses variable fan speed, depending on the need.

*Consumer Guide to Home Energy Savings* guided the selection of appliances and equipment. Sue has a front-loading washing machine and no dryer. The refrigerator is ultra

quiet, and she incorporated restaurant equipment to complete the kitchen.

### Space

This open plan is ideal for a single-person household and for the facilitation of airflow for heating and cooling. Additional space for guests and a work studio is located in the loft. A 20 x 20 covered porch extends the living area.

### Indoor Environmental Quality

Because Sue, like many of her clients, is chemically sensitive to synthetic substances and off-gassing vapors, all materials and finishes in the home were to be free of VOCs and formaldehyde. This is an area where experimentation revealed important information. A natural sealer selected for the solid wood cabinets contained natural terpins, which were not advertised by the supplier. While this is a naturally occurring substance, they are a VOC and need to be avoided. Although healthy products were locally available, there were occasions where subcontractors brought inappropriate caulks and sealants to the job site. It required meticulous attention and supervision to ensure that proper products were used. This was more an issue of education than availability. With the exception of one cabinet sealer that was mailed, everything was available locally over the counter. ■

# TOLLGATE CABIN:
# Building to Site

This cabin for the family of a local musician is a woodland retreat near the main residence (a large, restored eighteenth-century house). The site is pristine with large and mature hardwoods overlooking a small valley. This included an ancient beech, the drip line of which became the limit of the site disturbance.

The couple, with two small children, had a clear vision of what they wanted their home to be. Their main priority was to build a cabin in the woods without harming the beautiful landscape that enticed them, especially the magnificent eighty-year-old beech tree. This was to be a place to enjoy solitude and music, and where the kids could roam safely. The house had to feel as if it belonged there. Additionally the materials, energy use, water systems, landscaping, and, of course, views, all had to tell the same story of a return to and experi-

ence of natural systems. Their program called for about 2,700 square feet of space with an open, interconnected and informal feel. A small kitchen, play areas, and art, music, and exercise studios, formed an unusual set of requirements.

The owners hired an architect whom they felt would respond appropriately to these requirements. They found Tom Fisher through his work in green residential design, specifically

**Location:** Albemarle County, Virginia
**Architect:** Thomas A. Fisher, AIA, Environ Design Collaborative with Jen Cline, Assoc. AIA
**Owners:** Anonymous
**Square Footage:** 2,600
**Builder:** SPN Construction Managers; Jeff Smith, Mike Truslow and Rod Timmek, Supervisors
**Cost:** $200 per sq. ft.
**Photographer:** Philip Beaurline

## SUSTAINABLE FEATURES

- Minimized construction impact
- Construction waste management
- Compact site responsive design
- Passive solar design
- Integrated comfort strategies
- Use of recycled, healthy, and durable materials
- Use of earth wall system

LEFT

*The owners' vision of a weekend retreat was realized in the design of a cabin in the woods. Site sensitivity was a high priority and was accomplished by the stepped building form and preservation of the existing vegetation.*

BELOW

*Large windows connect the owners to the pristine forest while antique furnishings and natural tones create a comfortable setting for relaxation.*

from his design of a local store that specialized in ecologically responsive building materials. Tom had also coauthored the recent book on European ecological residential design: *Living Spaces*.

### Site

Central Virginia is a mixed climate with warm humid summers and mild winters with occasional snow. Passive solar gain strategies work well here, thus window sizes and calculated overhangs are key components to solar energy strategies. With the slope direction almost due west downhill, the architect worked to make the south-facing sides of the stepped structure perform for heat gain control. Also, with large deciduous trees very close to the structure it was easy to arrange for shade in the summer and plenty of light penetration during the winter. Depending on the orientation, glass was designated for each window as having low-E coatings on the inside, the outside, or none at all. This strategy handled the differing solar impacts as the sun moved across the house.

The site proved to be exceptionally challenging, with a nearly 30 degree slope and the owner's requirement that as many large trees be left as possible. The building form is integrated with the site by stepping down the hill while keeping the lower entry at the same contour elevation as the soapstone-and-wood walkway from the main house. The upper entry is just below the parking area and drive, which is cut into the slope with timber retaining walls. Cedar and stone exterior materials further help to visually merge the building with the site. Earthen greens and dark gray trim

and stains were used to blend with the natural colors of the area.

Native vegetation is artfully reintroduced or replanted right up to the foundation walls. Nearby trees, including the old beech, were carefully pruned by arborists. With no lawn, the house is nestled in the landscape and surrounded by rhododendrons, dogwood, rock outcrops, and the surrounding poplar, oak, and beech forest. No irrigation system is installed. To reabsorb runoff on-site, downspouts were avoided and the perimeter of the dwelling designed as a combination swale-and-gravel rain garden. Trees that were cut became part of the terraced landscaping. The old beech became the termination of an axis that began at the original house, passed through the lower studio, and ended as a deck at the rocks at the foot of the tree.

### Materials

Natural finishes, textures, and colors were used wherever possible. A light, airy, open feeling was sought on the upper level. Dark, cozy, and warm treatments were developed on the lower level. Nontoxic and low VOC sealants, adhesives, paints, and sealers were used throughout. Antique furnishings and fixtures, such as an old locally quarried soapstone sink, add to the charm of the home and meet sustainable criteria.

### Space

The large downhill studio space extends out into the forest and overlooks a small stream in the valley below. Skylights with windows, doors, and decks on three sides give the effect of being in

TOP
*A window nook for one is an invitation to curl up with a good book while staying within reach of the family's activities.*

BOTTOM
*A stage within the great room sets the tone for fun and play.*

the trees with the ease of stepping out-side to exterior decks and walkway spaces. The upper rooms include a play area, bathroom, kitchen, dining alcove, and bedroom.

### Energy

The building consists of two systems. Part of the structure is built with solid logs. The other portion is constructed using 2 x 6 wood frame construction with blown-in cellulose insulation and weatherization meas-ures to reduce infiltration.

The crawl space is insulated at the perimeter walls, rather than between the floor joists. Insulation stuffed between floor joists is rarely installed well and is often compromised by wiring, piping, and other penetrations. This home's use of a semiconditioned crawl space is more efficient due to the continuous nature of insulation at the perimeter and around the footings.

The large-view windows were placed on southern exposure and are protected by generous overhangs and the foliage of the nearby deciduous forest.

Heating is provided by a high seer heat pump system and a Jotul stove—a highly efficient Swedish wood stove. Lighting demands are met with the use of compact florescent fixtures throughout.

This home provides the family with a fun, multiuse getaway. Its informal qual-ity, access to the outdoors, and space for activities bring them back often. They accomplished these goals while also being sensitive to the environment; the ancient beech stands in gratitude. ■

ABOVE

*The small kitchen meets the demands of the family and is open to the eating area and great room, providing a feeling of spaciousness.*

Photo © Angela Dean

# CONCLUSION

Will it matter in the end? In the history of human occupation on the planet, it is only within a short time period that we have had a negative impact due to individual and collective actions. The idea of the human race leaving a positive footprint may seem to be an oxymoron. When we look around it is easy to question how we could develop without causing destruction to our surroundings. Yet humans are a naturally occurring element of the environment, evolved over thousands of years. We have adapted to our climate, food source, and shelter and have developed survival skills in order to exist. What separates us from other life is our art, culture, and consciousness. It is not so much human existence that threatens natural systems, but the choices we make about the type of existence we will live.

Research for this book revealed a community network of talented individuals in the field of green design. These individuals acknowledge that building and living sustainably is essential to our survival—as designers, builders, home owners, and occupants of the planet.

Thinking sustainably means thinking of earth as our home. In our own dwellings, we can take out the trash and put it on the street to be picked up, never to be seen again. We can use electricity without filling our homes with the emissions that result from its generation. This doesn't mean, however, that we are unaffected by the results of our actions. By choosing to live sustainably, we acknowledge our role in the natural process or web of life. We are choosing to take no more than we can return and to manage our resources in a manner that will sustain us as well as others.

Designing and building a home is a very personal and potentially very rewarding experience. The end result is many years enjoying the fruit of your labors. As you design and build your sustainable home, the choices you have made hopefully will bring you more joy than you had imagined and will serve as an inspiration to others to build green.

I BELIEVE IT TO BE PERFECTLY POSSIBLE FOR AN INDIVIDUAL TO ADOPT THE WAY OF LIFE OF THE FUTURE . . . WITHOUT HAVING TO WAIT FOR OTHERS TO DO SO. AND IF AN INDIVIDUAL CAN OBSERVE A CERTAIN RULE OF CONDUCT, CANNOT A GROUP OF INDIVIDUALS DO THE SAME? CANNOT WHOLE GROUPS OF PEOPLES—WHOLE NATIONS? NO ONE NEED WAIT FOR ANYONE ELSE TO ADOPT A HUMANE AND ENLIGHTENED COURSE OF ACTION." —M. K. Gandhi

# RESOURCES

## Architects and Designers

Paula Baker-Laporte
Baker-Laporte & Associates
P.O. Box 864
Tesuque, NM 87574
Tel. 505-989-1813
www.bakerlaporte.com

Sue Barnett
Stewardship, Inc.
307 Camino del Barranca
Cypress Mill, TX 78654-9514
Tel. 830-825-3305

Gayle Borst, AIA
Stewardship, Inc.
2313 W. 8th Street
Austin, TX 78703
Tel. 512-478-9033
www.StewardshipArchitecture.com

Angela Dean, AIA
AMD Architecture
573 7th Avenue
Salt Lake City, UT 84103
Tel. 801-322-3053
www.amdarchitecture.com

Thomas A. Fisher, AIA
The Folsom Group / McGuffey Hill
330 South Pineapple Avenue
Sarasota, FL 34236
Tel. 941-365-7336
www.mcguffeyhill.com

Pamela Freund and Ken
  Anderson (Design-Build Group)
Environmental Design Group
Enterprise
P.O. Box 2482
Taos, NM 87571
Tel. 505-758-5642
www.edgearchitects.com

Pete Gang
Common Sense Design
145 Keller Street
Petaluma, CA 94952
Tel. 707-762-4838
www.commonsensedesign.com

Mary Kraus
Kraus-Fitch Architects, Inc.
110 Pulpit Hill Road
Amherst, MA 01002
Tel. 413-549-5799
www.krausfitch.com

Kelly Lerner
One World Design, Design and
Consulting
925 Avis Drive
El Cerrito, CA 94530
Tel. 510-525-8582
www.one-world-design.com

Paul Okamoto
Okamoto Saijo Architecture
18 Bartol Street
San Francisco, CA 94133
Tel. 415-788-2118
www.os-architecture.com

Peter L. Pfeiffer, AIA
Barley + Pfeiffer Architects
1800 West 6th Street
Austin, TX 78703-4704
Tel. 512-476-8580 x101
www.barleypfeiffer.com

Terry Phalen
Living Shelter Design
320 Newport Way NW
Issaquah, WA 98027-3119
Tel. 425-427-8643
www.livingshelter.com

Daniel Sagan and Alisa Dworsky
(Design-Build)
Terra Firma Inc.
P.O. Box 1
Randolph, VT 05060
Tel: 802-728-6401
mailbox@terrafirmavt.com

Jack Thomas Associates
1352 W. White Pine Canyon Road
P.O. Box 68039
Park City, UT 84068
Tel. 435-645-7515

Sandra Vitzthum, Architect
46 East State Street
Montpelier, VT 05602
Tel. 802-223-1806

## Builders

Jon Alexander
Sunshine Construction
8709 Forest Hill Place NW
Seattle, WA 98117-3938
Tel. 206-782-4619

Geoff Austin
Leeward Construction
1348 Grove St.
San Francisco, CA 94117
Tel. 415-931-2405

Boa Constructor Building & Design
Michele Landegger
Debrae Lopes
1069 Summit Road
Watsonville, CA 95076
Tel. 408-848-1117

Dennis Caulfield
1103 Blair Street
Salt Lake City, UT 84111
Tel. 801-557-2908

Fairway Construction
Chris Oddo
P.O. Box 728
Angels Camp, CA 95221
Tel. 209-736-4326
Fairway@strawbale.net

Doug Kohl
Kohl Construction
31 Campus Plaza Road
Hadley, MA 01035
Tel. 413-256-0321

Robert Laporte
P.O. Box 864
Tesuque, NM 87574
Tel. 505-984-2928
www.econests.com

Don Lucas
1030 6th Street
Boulder, CO 80302
Tel. 303-517-0828
jloule@aol.com

Frank Meyer
Thangmaker Construction
904 E. Monroe
Austin, TX 78704
Tel. 512-916-8100
www.hometown.aol.com/thang-maker

Bill Moore
William T. Moore Construction, Inc.
1335 Bonham Terrace
Austin, TX 78704
Tel. 512-445-2772
byrdmoore@worldnet.att.net

New Age Builders Inc.
Route 1 Box 1550
Buckingham, VA 23921
Tel. 434-969-4976
www.newagebuildersva.com

Oliver Custom Homes
Matt and Paul Oliver
11506 Pradera Drive
Austin, TX 78759
Tel. 512-250-5889

Ra Solar Company
Jim Vann
P.O. Box 512
Waitsfield, VT 05673
Tel. 802-496-9496

Mark Rohrbach
MWR Construction
45431 Southeast Edgewick Road
North Bend, WA 98045
Tel. 425-888-2348
www.mwrcompany.com

Semmes & Co, Builders
Turko Semmes
7360 El Camino Real Suite D
Atascadero, CA 93422
Tel. 805-466-6737
www.semmesco.com

Jeff Smith
Alterra Construction Management
640 Arrowhead Drive
Earliesville, VA 22936

Sandra Sunksen
Greensleeves, Inc.
3275 SW Lake Grove Ave.
Lake Oswego, OR 97035
Tel. 503-675-3536

South Mountain Co.
John Abrams
P.O. Box 1260
West Tisbury, MA 02575
Tel. 508-693-4850
www.somoco.com

Sugar Hollow Builders
4870 Sugar Hollow Road
Crozet, VA 22932
Tel. 434-953-8147

Scott Weston
Cedar Creek Builders, Inc.
North 16660 Right Fork Road
Hauser Lake, ID 83854
Tel. 208-773-5776

Steve Whipperman
Signature Builders
3354 South 1940 East
Salt Lake City, UT 84106
Tel. 801-259-9447

## Products

Chemical Specialties Inc.
*ACA-free treated lumber*
One Woodlawn Green
Suite 250
200 East Woodlawn Road
Charlotte, NC 28217
Tel. 800-421-8661
www.treatedwood.com

Cob Cottage Company
Box 123
Cottage Grove, OR 97424
Tel. 541-942-2005
www.deatech.com/cobcottage

Environmental Home Center
*Environmental building supply*
1724 4th Avenue South
Seattle, WA 98134
Tel. 206-682-7332
800-281-9785
www.environmentalhomecenter.com

Faswall
K-X Industries
P.O. Box 88
Windsor, SC 29856
Tel. 800-491-7891
www.faswall.com

Green Adviser
*Information and interactive tools
for green living, diets, places, and
products*
257 Park Avenue South
New York, NY 10010
Tel. 212-505-2100
www.greenadviser.org

ICF Web
*product guide and directory for
Insulated Concrete Form systems*
www.idfweb.com

Rammed Earth Works
101 S. Coombs, Suite N
Napa, CA 94559
Tel. 707-224-2532
www.rammedearthworks.com

Real Goods Solar Living Center
*Environmental building supply
and sustainable living products from
air cleaners to composting toilets*
13771 S. Highway 101
Hopland, CA 95449
Tel. 707-744-2100
www.realgoods.com

Straw Sticks and Bricks
*Environmental building supply*
1734 West B Street
Lincoln, NE 68522
Tel. 402-435-5176
www.strawsticksandbricks.com

The Structural Insulated Panel
  Association (SIPA)
P.O. Box 1699
Gig Harbor, WA 98335
Tel. 253-858-SIPA
(253-858-7472)
www.sips.org

## Websites

### General

Co-op America's National
  Green Pages
*directory of products and services
for people and the planet*
www.coopamerica.org

Environmental Building News
www.BuildingGreen.com

Environmental Design and
  Construction Magazine
www.EDCmag.com

General Green Building Links
www.ci.san-jose.ca.us/esd/GB-
LINKS.HTM

National Association of Home
  Builders Research Center
www.nahbrc.com

Natural Home Magazine
www.naturalhomemagazine.com

Rocky Mountain Institute
*resources and information on
sustainable living, building, and
transportation*
www.rmi.org

Sustainable Sources
*professionals and resources for
green building*
www.greenbuilder.com

www.directory.greenbuilder.com
*directory of green building pro-
fessionals, building materials,
conferences, real estate, and
printed resources*

www.greenbuilder.com
*free online access to Sustainable
Living Sourcebook, covering topics of water, energy, building
materials, and solid waste*

www.oikos.com
*resource for building products,
and informative articles on green
building*

www.sustainableabc.com
*directory of green building profes-
sionals, building materials, and
printed resources*

### Energy

Energy Efficiency and Renewable
Energy Network DOE (EREN)
www.sustainable.doe.gov

Home Energy Ratings
www.energystar.gov/default.shtml

HomePower Magazine
www.homepower.com

Residential Energy Services
Network (RESNET)
www.natresnet.org

U.S. Environmental Protection
  Agency's Energy Star Program
  and Resources
www.energystar.gov

### Indoor Environmental Quality

Environmental Defense
*reports on human exposure to
environmental chemicals*
www.scorecard.org

National Institute for
  Occupational Safety and Health
  (NIOSH)
*information on effects of various
chemical exposures*
www.cdc.gov/niosh/npg/npg.html

## Local Green Building Programs

Austin, Texas
www.ci.austin.tx.us/greenbuilder

Colorado
www.builtgreen.org

San Jose, New Mexico
www.ci.san-jose.ca.us/esd/gb-home.htm

Scottsdale, Arizona
www.ci.scottsdale.az.us/green-building

Seattle, Washington
www.ci.seattle.wa.us/light/con-serve/sustainability

## Books and Magazines

### General

*The Alternative Building Sourcebook*
Fox Maple Press
www.foxmaple.com

*Architectural Resource Guide*
ADPSR West Coast
P.O. Box 9126
Berkeley, CA 94709-0126
Tel. 510-845-1000
www.adpsr-norcal.org

E-Magazine
*environmental topics ranging from local to global concerns*
P.O. Box 2047
Marion, OH 43305-2047
Tel. 815-734-1242
www.emagazine.com

Grist Magazine
*daily news, articles, and columns on environmental topics*
811 First Avenue
Suite 466
Seattle, WA 98104
Tel. 206-876-2020
www.gristmagazine.com

*Guide to Resource Efficient Building Elements*
Center for Resourceful Building Technology
P.O. Box 100
Missoula, Montana 59806
Tel. 406-549-7678
www.crbt.org

Pearson, David. *The Natural House Book*. New York: Simon & Schuster Inc., 1989.

*Real Goods Solar Living Sourcebook*. Real Goods Trading Corporation, Ukiah, California, 1994.

### Design

Alexander, Christopher, et al. *A Pattern Language: Towns, Building, Construction*. New York: Oxford University Press, 1977.

Browning, William and Dianna Lopez. *A Primer on Sustainable Building*. Snowmass, CO: Rocky Mountain Institute, 1995.

*Shelter*. Shelter Publications Inc, 1973.

Suzanka, Sarah. *Not So Big House*. Newtown, CT: Taunton Press, 1998.

Van der Ryn, Sim. *Ecological Design*. Washington, DC: Island Press, 1996.

### Energy

Kachadorian, James, *The Passive Solar House*. Chelsea Green Publishing, 1997.

Wilson, Alex, Jennifer Thorne, and John Morrill. *Consumer Guide to Home Energy Savings*. Washington, DC: American Council for an Energy Efficient Economy, 1996.

### Indoor Environmental Quality

Bower, John, *The Healthy House*. New York: Carol Communications, 1989.

Dadd, Debra Lynn. *Nontoxic, Natural & Earthwise*. New York: St. Martin's Press, 1990.

Goldbeck, David. *The Smart Kitchen: How to Design a Comfortable, Safe, Energy-Efficient, and Environmentally Friendly Workspace*. New York: Ceres Press, 1989.

Baker-Laporte, Paula, et al. *Prescriptions for a Healthy House*. Gabriola Island, BC, 2001.

### Materials

Easton, David. *The Rammed Earth House*. White River Junction, VT: Chelsea Green Publishing, 2002.

Evans, Ianto, Michael Smith, and Linda Smiley. *The Hand-Sculpted House*. White River Junction, VT: Chelsea Green Publishing, 2002.

Green Spec: Product Directory with Guideline Specifications. Brattleboro, VT: Building Green, 2001.

King, Bruce. *Buildings of Earth and Straw*. White River Junction, VT: Ecological Design Press, 1996.

Magwood, Chris and Peter Mack. *Straw Bale Building: How to plan, design and build with straw*. Gabriola Island, BC: New Society Publishers, 2000.

Steen, Athena and Bill Steen. *The Straw Bale House*. White River Junction, VT: Chelsea Green Publishing, 1994.

## Site

Hemenway, Toby and John Todd. *In Gaia's Garden: A Guide to Home Scale Permaculture*. White River Junction, VT: Chelsea Green Publishing, 2001.

Lyle, John Tillman. *Regenerative Design for Sustainable*

*Development*. New York: John Wiley and Sons, 1996.
Mollison, Bill. *Introduction to Permaculture*. Tyalgum, Australia: Tagari Publications, 1995.

## Organizations

American Institute of Architects
resources to help find an architect and questions to ask
www.aia.org

American Solar Energy Society
www.ases.org

Architects Designers and Planners for Social Responsibility (ADPSR)
P.O. Box 11754
Berkeley, CA 94712-2754
Tel. 415-974-1306
www.adpsr.org

Certified Forest Products Council
721 NW 9th Avenue
Suite 300
Portland, OR 97209
Tel. 503-224-2205
www.certifiedwood.org

Crest
*energy efficiency, renewable energy, and sustainable living resources*
www.sol.crest.org

Development Center for Appropriate Technology (DCAT)
*alternative building code research and support*
www.dcat.net

Environmental Defense
www.environmentaldefense.org

Forest Stewardship Council
1155 30th Street NW
Suite 300
Washington, DC 20007
Tel. 202-342-0413
www.fscus.org

International Institute for Bau-Biologie and Ecology
Education and resources for healthy building
P.O. Box 387
Clearwater, FL 33757
www.bau-biologieusa.com

Northwest Earth Institute
*national network of discussion courses and resources on voluntary simplicity, deep ecology, sense of place, and choices for sustainable living*
www.nwei.org

Solar Energy International
P.O. Box 715
76 S. 2nd. St.
Carbondale, CO 81623
Tel. 970-963-8855
www.solarenergy.org

U.S. Department of Energy
*energy efficiency and renewable energy; informative fact sheets are available as well as professional resources*
www.eere.energy.gov

U.S. Green Building Council (USGBC)
*A coalition of the nations leaders in the building industry working to promote high performance buildings*
1015 18th Street, NW
Suite 805
Washington, DC 20036
Tel. 202-82-USGBC
(202-828-7422)
www.usgbc.org